PENNY ANTE AND UP

PENNY ANTE
AND UP

Oswald Jacoby

A DOLPHIN BOOK
DOUBLEDAY & COMPANY, INC.
GARDEN CITY, NEW YORK

1979

Library of Congress Cataloging in Publication Data
Jacoby, Oswald, 1902–
Penny ante and up.
1. Poker.   I. Title.
GV1251.J214   795.4'12
ISBN 0-385-11173-8
Library of Congress Catalog Card Number 76–40882

Contents

Contents

Introduction

This book was planned as a treatise on penny-ante or small-stake poker. As I got along with the writing it became appropriate not only to concentrate on penny ante but also to explain something about high-stake poker as well as delve into the game of Hold'em, which has become the country's most popular new form of the great American game.

Basically, all poker games have the same essence. There is money involved and there will be winners and losers. I see occasional advertisements for books that guarantee to teach you how to win at poker. Such books are complete frauds. The net result of any poker game is that the players as a group will wind up losing an amount equal to the expenses of the game. Clearly, if each and every player had read one of these books, there would still be a net loss. Not that poker books, including this one, won't help you.

I won't guarantee that this book will make you a winner, but I do guarantee that it will increase the fun you get out of poker and that if your fun comes from winning, it will increase your chance of winning in the long run.

You won't win every time you play, but there are plenty of poker players whose yearly poker balance is a plus one. Even in the smallest of games there will be some players who pay their share of the expenses and still show substantial annual profits.

There is one characteristic of penny-ante poker that is conspicuously absent from high-stake games. That is the really bad player.

PENNY ANTE AND UP

1

Setting the Stakes

Yes, there are bad players in high-stake games, but somehow or other they don't last. Sometimes they just run out of money. More often they get tired of supporting the winners and depart for greener pastures.

This business of losing too much can apply to the two- or three-dollar regular contributor to a small-stake game. Two dollars a week amounts to $104 a year, and even at today's prices $104 can buy a lot of groceries.

As regards high-stake poker, I have heard of a private poker club in New York where the members were all multimillionaires in the days when just one million dollars represented enormous wealth. They met twice a week and, while no one came close to going broke, players did get tired of losing and it became necessary to recruit new members. Finally they recruited a player who just happened to be very good. In one year he won so much money that the game broke up. The losers could afford their losses, but they just got tired of losing to him.

This one-man drain would not have broken up the game

if it had included a couple of regular losers. Even in a very high-stake game there may be a couple of players who enjoy the game so much that they don't mind making large contributions. Add one expert to their game, and it means nothing to them.

It is the marginal players—those who are accustomed to breaking even or maybe picking up a few dollars in the long run—who suddenly find that they have become losers and quit the game.

A Couple of Rules of Play

There are two sure ways to lose at poker. The first way is to play in too many hands. When you throw even one chip into the pot for no good reason you are just wasting your money. It makes no difference if it is a penny chip or a ten-dollar chip, it is wasted money.

The second way is to keep throwing new money in the pot when things are going badly. Remember, once you put a chip in the pot it represents an investment. It may have been a splendid investment when you put it in, but if the investment has gone sour, don't spend any more money to protect it.

This matter of stakes is just as important in penny-ante games. If you like to play in a game where you are likely to lose or win twenty or thirty dollars in a session, you will be bored stiff in a game where you will only win or lose five or ten. Of course, you can avert boredom by playing in every pot and pushing up your losses. It won't increase your winnings because you won't win.

On the other hand, if you find that your pluses and minuses are likely to be fifty or a hundred dollars, you will be unhappy with that stake, so whatever type game you do play in make sure that you are playing for the right amount of money.

Of course, there are players who may even enjoy losing. I remember cutting against a wealthy Greek—a very wealthy Greek—and his partner in a bridge game some years ago. The stakes were quite high to start with, but the wealthy Greek promptly asked me for an extra bet.

I accepted with the remark, "You know that I have much the better of the game, don't you?"

He replied, "Certainly, but think of the fun I will have if I am lucky enough to win the rubber."

I found out later that this man had a pet superstition. It seems that in one year he showed a gambling profit but that was the only year in which his business ventures had gone badly. He just didn't want that to happen again, and it never did.

Whatever stakes you play for in a poker game, there is a proper stake for you. It is one where there is enough money involved so you will try to win but not enough so that you will be really hurt if you lose.

If you get into a game where the stakes are too high for you, get right out. You just won't want to play at a disadvantage, and you certainly don't want to lose something you can't afford to pay.

Some forty years ago I got into a game that turned out to be too big for me. The game was high-low table stakes seven-card stud, and while the size of the game had not appeared too much for my means at that time, it turned out that the conditions were. I had to put up my first stack on the first hand when my holding was easily the best at the table but it returned no chips. A second stack went almost

13

as quickly as did a third and fourth. With my fifth stack things began to improve, and when we finally got to the last round of play I was well ahead but still nervous. Everyone had more chips than I had, but I got involved with an exceptionally good first six cards.

The seventh card improved my hand still further, but I did not have a cinch. Then, the man to my left announced "Tap." He had more chips than anyone and his remark meant that he was betting enough so that it would cost everyone all his chips to call.

I had a very proper call and would have won half the pot if I had called, but when it came around to me after three people had called I threw my hand away. I stayed out of the last three pots and quit a small winner, but at least a winner.

Conversely, if the game is too small for you, it is going to be boring to play. You will probably throw away some small amount of money and won't get any pleasure out of the game if you do win.

The rule is: Don't go back to either game!

2

Ideal Poker Games

There is little chance that the ideal poker game will ever take place. If it does, the odds are that before long someone will be suggesting changes. These changes may not appear to mean anything at all, yet any change will have one result. It will affect the size of your game. Maybe the change will make it smaller, but experience has shown that changes tend to have a reverse effect and make the game larger.

Don't kid yourself about this, poker is a game of skill. There is plenty of luck in poker and there may well be some lucky poker players, but luck tends to even up. This doesn't mean that because you have been unlucky for two or three straight sessions, you are due for good luck the next time.

Assign the luck factor the numbers 0 to 10. Then 5 will represent average luck. You play three sessions with your luck factors for those sessions being 0, 1, and 2. I don't care how well or how badly you play, you will have shown a loss for each of those sessions. Don't think that your luck will run 8, 9, and 10 the next three. Cards have no memory, and each new session brings its own new luck.

Your next seven sessions are about average so that your luck total for those seven sessions is 35. Your total for ten games is 38, which is the same 12 below average shown after the first three, but your average per session has risen from 1 to 3.8. Play ninety more average sessions. Your luck total for one hundred sessions will now be 488. You will still be 12 points low, but your average will have risen to an almost normal 4.88.

You haven't succeeded in getting back that early 12-point deficit in your luck, but a little extra ability will make you a winner.

Mark skill on that same 0 to 10 scale and make your skill 5.5. Your total skill for ten sessions has been 5 points above average, and it will continue to aid you with each additional game. In other words, skill is a constant help to you; lack of skill a constant drain on your resources.

If you are a consistent loser, you are being outplayed. You can remedy this by improving your game; or you can quit and take up duplicate bridge or some game where you don't have to gamble. Or you can make a mental balance sheet and find that the amount of fun you have had is well worth the money you have lost.

The *ante:* This is defined as chips placed in the pot before the deal. The deal ante should be large enough to discourage really tight play, but not so large that you have to play in every pot just to protect your ante.

The *limit:* This is the maximum amount that a player may raise the last bet. In penny ante and nearly all gambling-house games the limit is a specified number of chips. In certain high-stake games the limit may be the size of the pot or your table stake, represented by the chips you have on the table or some combination of both. For general purposes we will stick to what are called limit games.

16

In the best limit games there are two or even three limits. One limit for the first bet or first raise, a second and higher limit for the other bets in the early rounds, and a final limit for the last one or two rounds of betting.

Limit on the Number of Raises

Around the turn of the century my father used to play in a five-dollar-limit Saturday afternoon poker game at his club.

The ante was one dollar per player; the only game dealt was five-card stud, and while the action was fast, a two-hundred-dollar win or loss was very large. Then came a most unusual hand. Player A showed a ten. Players B and C showed jacks. B and C started raising back and forth and it became apparent that each one had another jack in the hole. Hence, player A had all the worst of it since if he did not improve, one of the others was sure to win the pot and the odds were a good deal more than two to one against him.

After about twenty raises A begged for mercy. B replied, "You are taking the worst of it with each bet you call. I have a pair of jacks and I am sure C has the same. Don't whine—just get out."

Not very nice for a gentlemen's club, but poker players don't have to be nice. In addition neither B nor C liked A.

A few more raises and A asked father what should be done about the situation.

Father replied, "They are certainly within their rights to keep on raising and you have to call or drop. However, there is nothing in the rules to force you to act hastily. Why not study your next call for an hour or two?"

After this suggestion the three players agreed on five

17

more raises after which the cards would be dealt out. I don't know whether the result was a triumph of justice or not, but player A drew out on B and C and won the pot.

Trouble like this should be avoided, and the best way to do it is simply to limit the number of raises during the course of one round of betting. The most common limit is three to five, but some people like to make the limit three per player. Of course, this last limit means that a great many more raises are possible.

When the rule of some total number of raises per round is in effect, there is a certain ploy available to players who get caught in the middle between two people who like their hands. Suppose our old friends A, B, and C and a fourth player named D are left in the pot. There is a limit of 10 chips and four raises per round. A bets the 10-chip limit. B and C call and D raises 10 chips. A promptly raises back for the second 10-chip raise, whereupon B raises 1 chip (the third raise), and C raises 1 chip more to end that round's action. Each player has contributed 32 chips to the pot. With four 10-chip raises they would have put in 50 apiece.

Of course no one held a gun to B and C's heads and forced them to call the first two 10-chip raises. The point is that each one felt he had enough equity to warrant staying, but at the same time each one had managed to invest 18 chips less than he would have to pay if he just called.

Table Stakes

Originally, poker was strictly a gambling game and a very dangerous one because it was played with no limit at all. As such it was a wonderful game for fleecing a sucker.

A typical story would involve a wealthy plantation owner who had just sold his cotton crop in New Orleans. He would get into a poker game and eventually pick up an almost unbeatable hand. Maybe a king-high straight flush in a game of draw poker. After several raises there would be just one other man left in the pot. This player would reach in his pocket, haul out a big roll of bills and say, "I bet that."

The roll would be counted and turn out to be some ten thousand dollars more than the victim had. It would be up to him to drop out of the pot unless he could produce something of value to call that bet. He would announce that his plantation was worth a hundred thousand. After much discussion it would be valued at eighty. By this time our victim would be steaming mad. Instead of just calling, he would write out a deed to the plantation, throw it into the pot, and announce that he was raising the extra seventy thousand.

Now it would be up to the other man to find seventy thousand dollars or the equivalent. Somehow or other the money would be found. He would call the bet, throw down an ace-high straight flush, and take the other man's plantation.

The table-stakes feature doesn't give the sucker real protection (P. T. Barnum said, "There's a sucker born every minute," and Wilson Mizner added, "And two to take him."), but it does keep him from losing too much in any one pot because in any one pot a player is only allowed to bet what he has on the table. A loser can replenish his table stake before the next deal, but he can't add to it during the course of play of any hand.

The table-stakes feature is a pretty good one to put into

any and all poker games. For one thing, it puts an automatic check on how much a player can lose in one pot. Thus, it is an important rule in all gambling-house games. The house doesn't like to get stuck, and this way if they do get stuck it is only because they have let a customer get chips on credit.

Pot Limit and Similar Table-stakes Variations

One bad feature of table stakes is that a player can bet all his chips any time he wants to do so. A game really gets out of hand when someone throws a couple of thousand chips into the pot that only amounted to a hundred chips when the big bet was made.

With pot limit you can only bet what is in the pot and only raise what is in the pot after you put in enough chips to call the last bet or raise. Now, take our 100-chip pot. You bet the size of the pot or another 100 chips. The next player wants to raise. He has to use 100 chips to call, which puts 300 chips in the pot, so he can raise 300 chips. A call of that raise makes a 900-chip reraise legal, so pot limit gets you up to your table stake pretty quickly.

Doubling

European games have a simpler form of increased betting. Each raise just doubles what the last raise was. This works out about the same as half-pot limit.

In all games of this type it is essential, if you want to keep the game from getting out of hand, to retain the table-stakes feature as a final limit.

In a penny-ante game if you shift from one-way poker to

high-low split games, you are likely to ruin your game. Players just don't learn that the fact that there are likely to be two winners in a pot does not mean that they can afford to play in nearly all pots. Remember that when you get involved in a one-way pot, you can be sure on many occasions that you have no chance to call and win. Once you get involved in a high-low split hand the "Hope springs eternal in the human breast" principle applies, and you never get out.

Buying and Selling Chips

A player may buy additional chips before getting a new hand, but he may not buy during the play of a hand. In some games a player may not take chips off the table at any time. Thus, if he gets too many chips in front of him, his only way to protect himself is to cash in and wait for the next game.

In other games a player may do what is called "rat-holing." He sells his surplus chips to another player or to the banker or just takes them off the table and puts them in his pocket. Losers don't like to see a winner put chips in the rat hole. It means they can't get even with one winning hand.

Side Pots

When only two players are left in a table-stakes pot the final limit is the number of chips in front of the man with what is sometimes called "short money." When there are several players with different numbers of chips there are complications. Specifically, each player can bet only the

21

chips in front of him, and once they are bet he remains in the pot to the end and shares as far as his money has gone. Other players continue to bet on the side until a second player is tapped (has all his chips in the side pot). Then a second side pot is started (on rare occasions there will be three or even more side pots).

Let's look at a possible multipot example in a pot-limit game of five-card stud with a 20-chip ante by the dealer and a first bet of 10 chips by player A. Players B and C call to make a total of 50 chips, and player D, who is down to a table stake of just 50 chips, calls and raises with his last 40 chips. He may say something such as, "I might just as well be broke as the way I am," but it doesn't matter what he says. His chips are all in and he will be in the pot to the end. Player E calls as do A, B, and C to make a pot with 270 chips in it.

These 270 chips will be known as the main pot. D who has put in all his chips will remain in until the finish and will win that pot if he has the best hand. The other players will continue to bet but only in side pots and only as far as their chips allow. Also, if one of them fails to call a side pot bet, he must throw in his hand and lose all equity in the chips he has previously bet. D has an advantage. He can't be driven out. This is somewhat compensated for by the fact that he can't drive anyone else out.

Let's carry on with A, B, C, and E. At this point A has more chips than anyone, B has 150 chips, C has 550 chips, and E 950. We aren't interested in how many chips A has since he can't get action for more than 950 of them.

The next card is dealt, and A bets 270 chips (the size of the pot). B calls for his 150; C and E call for the full amount. The first side pot is completed with 600 chips in it, and a second side pot has been started with 360 chips in it.

The total pot is now 1,230 chips. D is in for the first 270; B for that and the second 600.

C still has 280 chips. E still has 680. A has more than that but can only bet 680 since that is the number of chips belonging to the man with the second highest amount of money.

The main pot consists of 270 chips. The first side pot in which everyone but D is interested holds 600 chips. A, B, C, and E are interested in it, and D and B, who have no chips left, are in the pot to the finish although D shares only in the 270-chip main pot.

The fourth card is dealt. The total pot is now 270+600+350 or 1,230 chips, and A bets 680 chips to tap C and E.

C calls for his 280 chips, but E decides to save his last 680 and throws in his hand. The second side pot now consists of 360+560 or 920 chips. Only A and C are interested in it, and the fifth card is dealt.

There can be no more betting. The hole cards are turned up and the winners determined.

If A or C has the best hand, he sweeps the board. If B holds the best hand, he takes the main pot and the first side pot of 600 chips. The better hand between A and C picks up the 920-chip second side pot.

If D has the best hand, he wins the main 270-chip pot; B with the second-best hand would take the first side pot so that three men collect some chips.

A Remarkable Hand

Some forty years ago I was playing in a game at the home of the late Philip Hal Sims. Hal was undoubtedly the best player of the game of auction bridge, the game that

23

preceded contract. He was right near the top in the first days of contract and no slouch at poker.

The game was seven-card stud high-low pot limit. It was the last hand of the evening. The man with the fewest chips was dealt three eights and shoved in all his chips right away. Everyone had good starts also and somehow or other all chips went in before the next card was dealt. There was a center pot and five side pots with everyone in to the finish.

We might still be dividing pots if it hadn't turned out that the man with the three eights made a full house and won high, while a man who was involved in all six pots won low with a **6–4–3–2–A*** and high in all side pots with an ace-high flush so that the second man swept the board after giving the first man half of the center pot. That was supposed to be the last hand, but the five losers all wanted more action and the game continued on.

If anyone wants to know how I came out in that pot, the answer is, "This is my book and I had the flush and the low."

Bluffs

A bluff is a bet made when you are sure that you don't have the winning hand but hope to win the pot because no one will call your bluff.

There are two reasons to bluff. The first and strangely enough the unimportant one is to steal the pot.

The second and important one is to keep your opponents off balance so you will be called when you do have the best

---

* In this book the ace is counted as low in low poker and both high and low in high-low except when otherwise specified.

hand. Just remember: The man who never bluffs never gets full value out of his good hands.

Bluffing is almost nonexistent in penny-ante games. Not that the same principles don't apply in all games, but somehow or other an attempt to bluff with a quarter in a fifty-cent pot is not as likely to succeed as a twenty-five-dollar bluff in a fifty-dollar pot.

The winning poker player picks the time to bluff. He learns which players are most likely to be bluffed out and tends to make his bluffs against them. He goes one step further and learns the circumstances under which his intended victims are least likely to call.

The saying, "Never try to bluff a loser," is grounded in fact. Winners like to stay winners and can be bluffed—particularly near the end of a session. Losers want to get even and are likely to call all bets in desperation.

The larger the bet in relation to the size of the pot, the less desirable a call. Some forty years ago I made up a story about an American playing in a million-dollar table-stake game in Hong Kong. All the other players were Chinese, and each player had at least a million dollars' worth of chips in front of him. The game was draw poker and our hero was one of five players who drew cards. He drew to the **K–Q–J–10** of diamonds.

After the draw the first Chinese said, "Aw Moy." The interpreter explained, "He has just bet ten thousand dollars." The second Chinese said, "Wong." The interpreter said, "He has called."

It was the American's turn to act and as he squeezed his cards he saw that he had drawn a red spot card. Final inspection showed that it was the useless eight of hearts. He said, "Aw shit." Everyone threw his hand away and the interpreter said, "Your million-dollar bet has won the pot."

Before a lot of readers rise up to inquire how he could make a bet without actually placing his chips or money in the pot, I will explain that in some games a bet is only made if the chips are actually placed in the pot, but in many others a player who announces a bet has made it. This was one of those games.

Customs of the Game

By its very nature poker is a game of wile, artifice, and stratagem. Just how far this can be carried is a matter of custom of the game. In all games it is clearly proper to make a great fuss about calling a bet. The poker expression is to "Call crying." This doesn't mean that the weeper is really worried. Maybe he could well have afforded to raise but wanted to keep later players in the pot. Or a player can finger a bunch of chips before finally just putting in enough to call when he has no intention whatsoever of raising.

As stated in my Hong Kong story, some games don't consider that a bet has been made until the chips are in the pot. Whatever the game customs, it is important that you learn them thoroughly.

Customs of the Ideal Game

1. An announced bet is deemed to have been made.
2. A player who intends to raise should announce raising before actually doing so. He is bound by this statement.

3. A player is not supposed to act out of turn, but if he does act out of turn, he is bound by this action. Thus, if a player drops out of turn he has to drop in turn. If he bets out of turn and it is now checked to him, he must make that bet.

4. A player who announces, "I am betting blind," must really be blind. (A blind bet is made in stud when you haven't looked at your hole card, or cards; in draw when you haven't looked at your hand or your draw in the event that you bet after the draw.)

Then there are certain amenities that should be followed in an ideal game.

There is a rather high-stake-limit game that plays regularly in St. Louis. Some years ago the big winner raised before the draw, stood pat, and bet after the draw. Everyone dropped but one man who was obviously thinking of calling. The big winner said, "Don't call me. I've got the nuts."

The other player dropped and reached for the winner's hand as he threw it away. This was improper. You are not entitled to see a hand unless it has been called, but this man was a loser and grabbed it anyway.

He turned it over and discovered that the loud speaker had been bluffing. Another player turned to the bluffer and said, "You don't belong in this game, and you have just played your last hand with us."

There is no penalty for throwing your hand away out of turn except that you have thrown it away, but it is a habit to avoid because it affects the rights of other players. Sometimes, this can be devastating. As an example in a game of five-card stud: Player A, who shows an ace and three other

27

cards, checks; player B bets with a queen showing; player C, who shows a king, is thinking when A throws his hand away. Now if C has a king in the hole he can raise with impunity. Kings can't beat aces but they sure beat queens.

Rules for the Ideal Poker Game

1.   There must be an ante. Most games have an ante by each player plus a possible extra ante by the dealer. This leads to lots of arguments when it is disclosed that some player (or possibly two players) has forgotten to ante. Someone once explained to me that he had paid his way through college by failing to ante. This trouble can be eliminated if the dealer antes for everyone.

In dealer's-choice games there is likely to be a different ante for each game. In such a case you have to let all players ante, and the way to do this is to have each man place his ante in front of him—not in the center of the table.

2.   There should be two limits. First the maximum raise and second a limit to what a player can lose on any one hand.

3.   The limit should be greater for late rounds of betting than for the first or the early rounds. The ante and the limits should be of such a nature that players will play a good part of the time and that there will still be bluffing possibilities.

4.   In dealer's-choice games, the choice should be restricted to a definite set of games.

Suppose we want to develop our own poker game. We want it to be fast and interesting. We want the stakes to be enough to lend spice to the action without being too high

28

for any potential players. We want to encourage people to play in a good percentage of the pots without making the ante so high that everyone must stay with almost every hand.

So let's start with the ante. It should be either 1 chip per player or, simpler and more efficient, a 5- or 10-chip ante by the dealer.

The final and extreme limit should be 25 chips, but the limit bet would only be allowed in the last round of betting. The limit for the first and early rounds should be 5 chips.

There should be one other limit. The first bet would have to be just 1 chip.

If you want to play just one game, go ahead. If you want to play dealer's choice, decide just which games you want to allow and stick to them. Do not allow games that include too many rounds of betting. The reason for this is that pots take too long and players who had to drop out on the first round get bored waiting to get back into action.

HIGH-LOW

High-low split poker is almost like a habit-forming drug. Once you get started on it, you can't stop. I love this form of poker and always deal some split game when the house rules allow me to do so. At the same time, I must offer a strong word of caution. When you shift from either high or low poker to high-low split, you are just about doubling the size of your game. There are two reasons for this. The first is that more players tend to stay for the first round of betting. The second is that there are more raises. If you and I each think our hand is the winner in a game of just high or just low, it doesn't take long for one of us to decide he may be wrong. If you think you have the high and I think I have the low, we both keep raising as long as we can do so.

WILD CARDS

I recommend strongly that you stay away from wild-card games. They sound intriguing, and the man who wants you to play them is likely to say, "They make the game easier for everyone."

This statement rates somewhere between a lie and a damned lie. The only person wild cards make the game easier for is the man who understands them thoroughly. In other words, when you add wild cards you are increasing the expert's edge, not decreasing it.

They also tend to encourage loose play. A pair of aces is a pretty good hand in draw poker. Make the deuces wild, and a player with a pair of aces is likely to play it the same way he would in regular poker but with disastrous results.

Then wild cards complicate the game further. Put in a joker and people will argue as to whether joker plus A–10–8–6 of hearts is a double-ace flush and beats A–K–Q–6–4 of spades, or is just an A–K flush and loses.

Make deuces wild. Is 6–5–4–3–A a straight? Does five of a kind beat a straight flush?

ROODLES

In many games a round or two of roodles is played at the end. The ante is doubled or even increased further. Maybe the limit is raised also. In any event, the ostensible purpose of roodles is to give the losers a chance to get even. Usually it has the reverse effect and merely increases their losses. In any event, the less roodles you play the better off you are likely to be. They may be fun, but they aren't poker.

I remember my first experience with roodles as a mixture of horror and pleasure. A sudden summer storm had driven a bunch of us kids indoors in the middle of the afternoon. I was one of half a dozen eight-year-olds, and there were about the same number of teen-agers in the group.

Our host found cards and poker chips and the older children proposed a poker game. I asked to be allowed in. My father had already taught me basic rules for play in draw and five-card stud, and like nearly all people who like to gamble I was and still am an optimist.

I was told that everyone who played would have to put up ten cents. I happened to have a dime (all my worldly wealth at that point in time) and my next week's allowance of another dime was due in a couple of days, so I got into the game.

We played a simple game of draw poker with jacks or better to open. We were going to stop at five, at which time the big winner would get 40 cents out of the 80 cents produced by eight dimes. The next man would collect 20 cents, the next two get their money back, and the other four lose their dimes.

At ten minutes to five I was the big winner and envisioned the wealth that 40 cents represented. Then, the dealer said, "A round of roodles. Aces to open; everyone ante ten chips."

For the last hand dealt at five o'clock there were several hands passed out when no one could open. Each required another ante. I took stock and saw that I had to play in this last pot to stand any chance of getting the 40 cents I wanted, and that it wouldn't bankrupt me to play and to draw five cards if necessary. I was going to get my dime back regardless of who won the pot.

So the pot was opened and raised. I stayed with a pair of eights, drew three cards and still remember the thrill of looking at the three kings that the dealer gave me. I went home an eight-year-old millionaire.

I don't recommend roodles, but if you must play them, restrict them to one round. If you don't, you have just doubled or trebled the size of your game.

Blind Bets

In all forms of poker except those draw games where a certain minimum holding is required to make the first bet, the first man to act may bet blind—without seeing any of his cards. Some games even have a compulsory blind bet. In addition, if the first man bets blind, the next player may straddle by raising blind.

I remember a pot-limit game of lowball where the dealer anted 10 chips. The game went into overtime, and we added a compulsory blind opening of 10 chips. A little later on we started having the second man play for 20 chips. All this changed the complexion of the game. It had suddenly grown from a moderate game to a very high-stake game. Worse was yet to come. Player three shoved in 40 chips as the deal started and announced, "I'll raise to forty blind."

In the excitement the dealer failed to give him any cards. I noticed this and asked the 40-chip bettor, "Are you really blind?"

He said, "Are you doubting my honesty?"

I asked, "If you are really blind where is your hand?"

In some games the blind bettor is given the right to raise when it gets back to him if no one has raised his blind bet. This extra feature increases the size of the game a trifle more and slightly reduces the blind bettor's disadvantage.

It also leads to interesting plays. For example, as dealer in a draw game that includes this feature you find yourself with a very good hand. No one raises and you just call because you know that this blind bettor is likely to take advantage of this special right to raise. Sure enough he does. Several people call, and now you have your harpoon ready and strike.

Special Hands

In some draw-poker games additional hands are played in order to liven the game. The more common ones are:

The Big Dog: An ace and a nine plus three intermediate cards.

The Little Dog: A seven and a deuce plus three intermediate cards.

The Big Tiger: A king and an eight plus three intermediate cards.

The Little Tiger: An eight and a trey plus three intermediate cards.

The Kilter: A nine, five, and deuce plus two intermediate cards.

The Cat-hop or -skip Straight: Such as **10–8–6–4–2.**

Of course, a pair ruins any one of these hands.

When any of these hands are played, the kilter ranks

33

above three of a kind and below a straight. The dog ranks above a straight; the tiger above a dog and the cat-hop above a tiger. All rank below a flush.

These special hands are only used in draw poker, and I will come back to them when I discuss that game.

The Lallapalooza

An expert player got into a high-stake game in a gambling house. He played cautiously until he finally picked up a royal flush. To his great pleasure he got all his chips into the pot; in fact, he finally called the last bet and showed his hand. The other player showed a **J–8–7–5–3** of four different suits and reached for the pot. When the expert objected, they showed a picture of the hand on the wall with the proviso, "A lallapalooza is the highest hand."

Our man replenished his stack and picked up a lallapalooza about an hour later. All his money got in; he reached for the pot and was shown a second sign, "Only one lallapalooza is good a night."

Of course there is no such hand as the lallapalooza, and the story merely goes as a further warning to be sure you understand all the conditions of whatever game you play in.

What to Avoid in Poker Games

Suppose you are invited to play in an existing poker game. In general, go ahead and play. However, even though the players are all good friends of yours, there are lots of things you should watch for:

1. How is the game settled? The best rule is that when

a man stops he either pays if he is a loser, or collects from a loser if he is a winner. Then at the end of play, all losers pay right then and there. Any system that allows deferred pay leads to eventual trouble.

2. Is there a definite quitting time that is adhered to? When you play overtime not only do the winnings and losings mount astronomically, but the players are unhappy the next day.

3. What are average and big winnings and losings in the game? Make sure that the game is large enough to amuse you and not large enough to hurt you.

4. If a limit game is played, are players allowed to go light in pots? There is no apparent harm in this, but lots of potential real harm. I remember one nice limit game I played in in the twenties. One old man known as "Doc" hated to buy extra chips. If his stack melted away, he would go light in a pot or pots if he won the first short pot. This wouldn't have been bad except that he was very forgetful. He would go light on one round of betting and then use the chips he was light with as betting chips on the next round.

Someone usually corrected this, but I did notice that when he bought a new stack and made good his light chips he tended to underpay and got away with quite a few chips.

I didn't say anything about this until after the game. His small peccadillos hadn't hurt me, and I didn't feel it was appropriate for a youngster playing for the first time to comment.

I did ask afterward and was told, "Doc always loses anyway. He is a delightful man; loves to play; may not even know he is underpaying; and we just let him save these few chips."

35

Except for that rare poker game played for cash or gambling-house games where players buy their chips from a cashier and sell them back when they quit, records must be kept and the game settled at the end of play.

To do this, one player is selected to act as banker. He distributes the chips at the start of play, sells or gives out extra chips when required, and cashes in chips at the finish. No matter how careful the bookkeeper is, there are likely to be errors. The players are generally required to share responsibility for errors, and there is no trouble when it appears that more money has been lost than won so the books show a profit. It doesn't work out this way very often. Most of the time the books show a loss that someone has to make good.

This is usually done by an assessment against the winners. In a game that plays regularly, it is also possible to carry the loss forward to the next session and kitty out to make it up.

The best way is to keep those errors to a minimum. To do this, I suggest that the banker follow these procedures:

1. Chips are sold in units of one stack. Transactions involving a fraction of a stack should be strictly forbidden.

2. All transactions should be between the banker and a player. Never between two players.

3. Transactions should be kept to a minimum. In limit games give each player enough chips so that he won't be coming back to buy more every few minutes. In table-stakes games sell each player his stack plus several markers. These can be chips of a special color, mah-jongg counters, or anything else that is distinctive. A player turns in a marker for chips whenever he wishes but will be responsible for them at the end of the game.

36

4. If further precautions are deemed necessary, require each player to sign for chips any time he buys some.

The Kitty

In a very few poker games the host takes care of the expenses. Such games are few and far between. In others the players kitty out for expenses. In gambling-house games the kitty is apt to be quite large. After all the house has to show a profit. Even here there are reasonable and unreasonable charges. The best way, from the standpoint of the player, is the flat fee; the next best, the flat fee repeated at certain regular intervals.

The most popular way of covering expenses from the standpoint of the house is where chips are taken from each pot over a certain size. Here the kitty is apt to be huge, yet the unthinking player doesn't realize how much he is contributing for the privilege of playing.

In your own game the first step in determining the kitty is to decide which expenses shall be charged to the game and which to the players. Then kitty out to cover these expenses while you let each player handle his own extra charges.

I strongly recommend that all or most of the expenses be taken care of by the players each paying a flat amount. When you kitty out of pots you are charging the liberal player who is in action most of the time a lot while letting the tight man get away lightly. Since tight players lend little except their actual presence to a game, it is the liberal players who make it work. Why penalize them?

3

Draw Poker

The original poker game was sometimes called "Bluff." Each player was dealt five cards, one at a time. The players, starting at the dealer's left, either bet or threw their hands away. Anyone could get out, call, or raise, and betting continued until the last bet or raise was called or until no one called the last bet.

The game was played as either table stakes or no limit, and it got its name from the prevalence of bluffing.

Except for the gambling element it was rather boring, and it didn't take long for some genius to discover that if a draw feature and second round of betting were added, the game really improved.

This new game was called "Draw Poker." The first man to bet is known as the opener, and after one round of betting the players, starting with the opener, discard as many of their five cards as they want to, and receive new cards to replace them. A second round of betting followed by a showdown ends the hand.

Dealer's Advantage

The player to the dealer's left must act first and the dealer always gets to act last. In passout, where the players must either bet or throw their hands away, the dealer may actually win the antes without having to bet.

In other games a player may check and retain the right to back in or even raise if some later player opens.

Jackpots

This very popular form of poker requires that the opener hold a pair of jacks or better. Jackpots may also be played with other minimum requirements such as a lower pair, higher pair, or even two pair.

The best jackpot game as well as other poker games is seven- or eight-handed, and I am going to discuss such a game.

But before going further, take a look at the tables on the next page.

Table II is the important one. It shows clearly that you can't afford to pass with a pair of aces in any position and really shouldn't pass with a pair of kings. As for queens and jacks you should certainly open in one of the later seats but definitely should not open with jacks in first or second seat or queens in first seat.

Of course, if several hands have been passed out and additional antes made, it pays to open any time you can do so. Your percentage has improved considerably.

40

TABLE I

POSSIBLE POKER HANDS IN A
FIFTY-TWO-CARD PACK

	Actual Number Possible	Expected Number in 10,000 Deals	Approximate Number of Times	
Straight flush	40	⅙	Once in 64,974	deals
Four of a kind	624	2½	Once in 4,165	deals
Full house	3,744	14	Once in 694	deals
Flush	5,108	20	Once in 509	deals
Straight	10,200	39	Once in 256	deals
Three of a kind	54,912	211	Once in 48	deals
Two pairs	123,552	475	Once in 21	deals
One pair	1,098,240	4,226	Once in 2½	deals
No pair	1,302,540	5,012	Once in 2	deals
Total	2,598,960	10,000		

TABLE II

CHANCES OF HOLDING ANY PARTICULAR
HAND OR BETTER IN FIRST FIVE CARDS

	Approximate Number of Times	Exact Chance
Any pair or better	Once in 2 deals	.4988
Pair of jacks or better	Once in 5 deals	.2062
Pair of queens or better	Once in 6 deals	.1737
Pair of kings or better	Once in 7 deals	.1412
Pair of aces or better	Once in 9 deals	.1087
Two pairs or better	Once in 13 deals	.0762
Three of a kind or better	Once in 35 deals	.0287
Straight or better	Once in 132 deals	.0076
Flush or better	Once in 270 deals	.0037
Full house or better	Once in 588 deals	.0017

The chance of holding any specified pair is .0325.

41

Sandbagging

Sometimes you want to pass with a good hand. If no one opens, you have lost a few chips that you would have picked up. If someone else opens, you get a chance to raise and build up a nice pot.

You should have at least three of a kind to sandbag, and you should have mostly low cards. Thus, if you are dealt three kings, there is no chance that someone else will have a pair of kings. If you are dealt three kings, an ace, and a jack, the chance of finding another man with a pair of jacks or aces is reduced. On the other hand, if you pick up a small set of three and two odd low cards or a small straight or flush, there is a really good chance that someone will walk into your trap.

The tightest penny-ante game I have ever seen was the Admiral's game at Panmunjom. Vice Admiral Turner Joy, the head of the United Nations delegation, would hold a game in his tent about once every two or three weeks. I got into the game as SPPP (senior poker player present). Other players were either of flag rank or senior colonels and captains who would be getting flag rank shortly.

It wasn't penny ante. It was nickel ante, quarter limit, with three raises each round. They played nothing but straight jackpots, and while you were allowed to open for a quarter it was customary to open for a dime, and as the junior officer in the game I wasn't going to stir things up.

The three-raise limit didn't make much difference. I did see the full quota of three before the draw and three after the draw when two flushes and a full house were dealt pat.

42

Five dollars would be a substantial win or loss, and I feel sure that if I had ever won over ten dollars in a session it would have caused considerable comment. The game didn't last long. It convened at 2000 hours (8 P.M.) and stopped with a final round at 2200 hours (10 P.M.).

The Draw

Most of the time, it pays to draw down to your hand. In other words, if dealt a pair, draw three cards; if dealt three of a kind, draw two.

When you hold a kicker your chances of improving go down. Thus, when you draw down to a pair the odds against your making some improvement are 2½–1. When you hold a kicker they go up to 3–1.

When you hold a kicker to three of a kind the odds against your improving are almost 11–1; when you draw two cards these odds against you are just 8½–1.

Then why should you hold a kicker? The first and main reason is that you don't want to tell your opponents everything about your hand. Don't hold kickers all the time, but hold them often enough so that when you draw two cards your opponents will have to guess whether or not you hold three of a kind.

You should also draw just one card to three of a kind when you feel like it. This will make it a trifle harder for your opponents to read your one-card draws.

Occasionally a player will stand pat with two pair. There is enough reason to do this so that I suggest if you play every day, you try this about once each five years. The rest of the time draw and try to make that full house.

43

What to Draw To

This depends on what you have to put in to get into the pot and what you stand to win. It also depends on whether or not the pot has been raised before it is up to you to bet or drop. The general rule is to draw to kings or better.

Queens and jacks are doubtful hands to play, and as for lower pairs (sometimes called shorts) the less you spend on them the better your financial standing.

Drawing to a Four Flush

This is a very popular draw and deservedly so. Nine cards out of the forty-seven you haven't seen will make your flush, so that the odds against your making it are only a trifle over 4–1. If you miss your flush, you don't lose anything more. If you make it, you figure to pick up a lot of chips.

Drawing to Straights

The draw to an open-end straight is not as desirable as the draw to a flush. Only eight cards make your straight, so the odds against you are just about 5–1. Then, if you make it and someone else makes a flush, he will beat you.

As regards the draw to an inside straight such as **8–7–6–4,** the thing to remember is that you have just one chance in twelve of making your straight, and if you do make it, there is no guarantee that you will win the pot. As some Shakespeare of poker once wrote:

> He who draws to an inside straight
> Will hang his hat on the poorhouse gate.

44

Freak Draws

Four- and five-card draws and two-card draws to a straight flush are essential if you want to play in every pot. They are also likely to be losing propositions. Don't feel impelled to make them.

Changing Your Draw

Two stories are appropriate here. The first one concerns my father playing in a limit game. The pot was opened by the fifth seat, and Father, in seventh seat, raised with **8-8-4-4-A.** The opener called the raise and drew one card, whereupon Father threw away his pair of fours and drew to the two eights and ace kicker.

This was really good strategy. The opener would have raised back with aces up or three of a kind. He almost surely would have dropped with two very little pairs. Hence, Father could expect to win with aces up or three eights. The odds against making aces up or better on this draw were only 3–1. The odds against drawing one card and making a full house were 11–1.

The other concerned the late Bill Bagby of Dallas. Bill was a very good and very observant player. In a pot-limit game he saw the player to the dealer's left open after looking at only three cards. Bill's hand was the **K–Q–J–7–6** of hearts. He raised; the opener raised back; Bill tapped since by this time the size of the pot had reached the table stake. The opener called and stood pat.

It was obvious to Bill that the opener held a full house, so Bill threw away his **7–6** of hearts and tried for the straight flush. He didn't make it, but at least he had given the cards a chance.

Raising Before the Draw

You should raise with jacks up or better and when the pot is opened in one of the late seats with any two pair. Aces up, or maybe even kings up, are worth a reraise as are a small three of a kind. A large three of a kind is worth a third raise; a straight, a fourth raise; a flush, a fifth raise; and so on.

In games where the ante is very large in relation to the limit, you raise even more freely; when the ante is comparatively small, become a trifle more snug.

Splitting Openers

With several players in the pot and particularly in a raised pot, it is good policy to split openers if you hold a four flush. Your flush will be a very probable winner, two pair or even three of a kind are not too likely, while you can be sure that your one pair won't win.

You may even split to draw to an open-end straight, although this latter policy is not recommended except under exceptional circumstances.

Betting After the Draw

This is usually a matter for "at the table" judgment. You bet if you think someone will call and lose to you. You don't bet merely because your hand has improved.

Suppose you open as dealer with a pair of aces. If one man stays with you and draws three cards, you should bet out if you have made any improvement. On the other hand, suppose one, two, or maybe three players have stayed and drawn one card each.

You look at your draw and are pleased to see that a third ace has joined its brothers. Still, there is no reason to bet. Obviously, they were all drawing to flushes or straights. No one who hasn't hit is going to call your bet, and you have nothing to gain by making it.

PASSOUT OR GUTS

In this game you can't check before the draw. In other words, if you pass, you passout. You can open on anything and many players tend to open for one chip to save their right to play on. Beware—when a good player does this, he is very likely to be sandbagging.

In general, it does not pay to open with shorts under the guns. When you sit near the dealer you should open quite light, and when right next to the dealer it pays to open on occasion with nothing at all. A bet gives you a good chance to pick up the ante.

The late R. H. ("Buzz") Venable of Dallas, one of the richest, best, and funniest players I have ever had the pleasure of playing with, used to claim that the man to the dealer's left should always bet. His reason was that you just couldn't let the dealer grab the ante without some competition. Not that Buzz did bet every time in this position— merely that he thought all *other* players should.

Blind Openings

A blind opening is one made before you have seen your cards. In some games, including most gambling-house games, there is a compulsory blind opening.

47

Occasionally, as an inducement to a player to open blind, he is given the right to raise even though no one has raised his blind bet. In any event, blind openings lead to one result. The size of the game is just about doubled.

Bluffing

The more you can bet in relation to the size of the pot, the more chance there is for a bluff to succeed and the more bluffs made. The most successful bluffs are the pat-hand bluffs. You stand pat and bet. One way is to open with queens or jacks. You figure that the person who has called has you beaten, so you stand pat and bet out.

A more sophisticated pat-hand bluff is just to call the opener. Then, after he draws stand pat. When you bet out he is likely to feel certain that your failure to raise was based on the hope that someone else would raise and give you a chance to reraise.

Some years ago I was playing in a 25-chip-limit game with a 40-chip ante. It was also customary for all bets to be for the limit. The first player opened and the second man called. Player three raised, and when I looked at my cards I held an ace-high flush. There was no reason to raise. I wanted competition so I just called. Everyone dropped until it got back to the opener who raised back. The next man dropped; the raiser called; I raised; the opener raised and I gave what turned out to be the last raise. Thus, there were 515 chips in the pot before the draw.

The opener stood pat, the raiser drew two cards, and I stood pat. Both players checked and I bet another 25 chips. The opener called and now the man who had drawn two cards raised. This put a total of 615 chips in the pot of

48

which 175 were mine, but no more of mine went in. I knew I had the opener beaten, but I also knew that the man who had drawn two cards had made either a full house or four of a kind.

Anyway, the opener was the sort of man who was going to call, and I would get to see what the draw had brought forth.

Incidentally, while my last bet had cost me 25 chips, it had been the correct action. I knew I had the opener's pat hand beaten, and I knew he would call. I might even get a call from the two-card draw, and the odds against his improving had been 8–1.

There was a strange final result. The opener was really mad at me and blamed me for the loss of the 50 chips he had put in after the draw.

LOW-DRAW POKER (LOWBALL)

This is one of the really popular forms of poker. Lots of people want to play lowball and nothing else, and there are plenty of lowball games around for devotees. It can be played for high stakes or low stakes. Either way, it is a game where action should be encouraged by a fairly large ante, a compulsory blind bet with a limit before the draw of either the blind bet or twice the blind bet, and a further double for the after-the-draw limit.

This leads to rather liberal play. You can't sit back and wait for the nuts since the ante and the compulsory blind bets will break you. In spite of this, lowball is still a game of pat hands and one-card draws.

Lowball may be played with **7–5–4–3–2** or **6–4–3–2–A,** the best low, but in this book we assume that while a pair ruins a low hand, straights and flushes don't count against you and the best low is **5–4–3–2–A,** sometimes called the wheel.

The following tables are instructive.

Chance of holding various pat hands:

Wheel (five low)	.0004
6 low or better	.0024
7 low or better	.008
8 low or better	.028
9 low or better	.055
10 low or better	.099
Jack low or better	.182

If you throw a king from **K–A–2–3–4** your chance to make various low hands is:

Wheel	.085
6 or better	.170
7 or better	.255
8 or better	.340
9 or better	.425
10 or better	.511
Jack or better	.596

These tables clearly show why you should not stand pat with a jack low. It also shows why a ten low is barely playable, and even nine lows are nothing to burst into paeans of joy about.

Two-card Draws

Two-card draws are another low-poker luxury. If you discard your kings from **K–K–A–2–3** your chances of making various low hands are:

Wheel	.015
6 or better	.044
7 or better	.089

50

8 or better	.15
9 or better	.22
10 or better	.31
Jack or better	.41

These chances are slim ones indeed. It is almost 6–1 against making as good as an eight low. Then, when should you draw two cards?

The first time is when you have been forced to bet blind and no one has raised you.

The second is when you can get into the pot very cheaply.

The final instance is when you have been planning to stand pat with **9–8–5–3–2** or something similar, and realize that another player has a better pat hand. You definitely chuck the **9** and may well throw the **8** also in an effort to come up with a real winner.

Betting After the Draw in Lowball

You tend to bet right out with a seven low or better, to bet about half the time with an eight, and to restrict your action with a nine low or worse to just calling if someone else bets. In this last instance, you only call because you suspect a bluff or because the conditions of the game are such that players do tend to bet out with nines.

Bluffing

You can't play good lowball unless you do a fair amount of bluffing. Not so much that you always get called but enough so you will get a lot of proper bets called.

Most bluffing situations occur when there are only one or two other players left in the pot. The most common one is

51

when you have drawn one card and your one opponent has drawn two. My own rule here is to bet when I have made a pair of threes or worse. The two-card-draw man is not going to call me with a lower pair and is quite likely to drop with a king, queen, or jack low.

In this game more than any other you should learn who can be bluffed and who can't, or better, who is likely to be bluffed and who isn't.

Bluffing does not mean much in penny ante. Somehow or other you are going to be called when you bluff in small-stake lowball unless it turns out you are bluffing with the best hand. This does happen. You draw one card—make a pair—and bluff. The two-card draws have produced two pairs and three of a kind and can't and don't call.

4

Draw-poker Variations

This chapter will cover some of the many draw-poker variations you may run into in different games. They are all interesting; most of them tend to add extra zest to the game and increase both its size and its complexity.

JACKS AND BACK OR UP AND BACK

The players in turn have the right to open for high provided they wish to do so and have proper openers. If no one opens for high, the game reverts to lowball passout.

It can be a most frustrating game. You are dealt a very good low hand such as **6–4–3–2–A.** The high betting gets around to the dealer who opens and ruins your dreams of sugarplums.

It can also be very rewarding. You pick up a wheel. Naturally enough you don't open for high where your pat hand is unlikely to win much of a pot. If someone else opens for high, you get a chance to raise; if no one opens for high, you are playing lowball with a sure winner.

53

The up-and-back game seldom gets back to low. Somehow or other when you have a really good hand someone opens for high. This shouldn't happen because your requirements to open in an early seat should be just about the same as if you needed jacks or better. The only exception is that you should open with a four flush. Sandbagging works well here because some late player will open to try to steal the ante.

Once in a blue moon some player will deal low and back to high. Offhand it looks like a good game, but in practice, it tends to become straight lowball.

SHOTGUN

In this version of draw poker each player is dealt four cards and there are three rounds of betting. The first round is passout. You either bet or get out. Those who remain in get a fifth card, and the second round of betting follows. Then there is a draw followed by the third and final round.

The dealer has a great advantage since he gets to bet last in each round.

Shotgun can be played for high, low, or high-low split. It can also be played as two- or three-card shotgun or as double-barreled shotgun.

In three-card shotgun you get three cards, bet; get a fourth card, bet; get your fifth card, bet; draw and bet once more.

Two-card shotgun is similar except that you start with just two cards.

In double-barreled shotgun you have four extra rounds of betting since you turn up your final hand one card at a time and bet after each turn. I have a strong recommendation about the double-barreled game: Shun it like the plague!

PENNY-ANTE SHOTGUN

This can be a great game if played with a large enough ante so that there will be plenty of proper action. When played with a small ante, the way to win is to play very tight.

POT-LIMIT SHOTGUN

I am only going to discuss the low game here. Frankly, high shotgun is not much of a game when played pot limit because it is just too dangerous. I will discuss both the four- and three-card games because each one is a good game. I will also assume a 5-chip ante by the dealer.

A player may bet the size of the pot, but it is good tactics for a player who opens in one of the first seats to bet just 1 chip. A player who opens right in front of the dealer should open for the size of the pot; sometimes even with a bad hand in an effort to pick up the ante.

It is a matter of percentage. If only the dealer is in back of you, he is quite likely to drop and let you steal the ante. Therefore, an alert dealer will be very suspicious if a good player sitting at his right opens for just 1 chip. He won't let that 1-chip bet drive him out, but he also won't let it encourage him to raise.

What to Play With

In first or second seat in four-card shotgun, your worst hand to play should be four cards to a nine low or three cards to a seven, and you won't be playing badly if you make these requirements even more severe. (It has been said there are old shotgun players and wild shotgun players, but no old wild shotgun players.) In later seats you can reduce these requirements a trifle.

In three-card shotgun your tendency should be to throw away any hand with one bad card and count nines as bad cards. Again, that is in first or second seat. If the pot has not been raised, the dealer can stay with any two good cards.

When to Raise or Reraise

In the four-card game the dealer should raise with four cards to a seven; the man to his right should do the same most of the time. The exception might be if the dealer is a wild player and likely to raise with just a fair hand. In that case, it may pay to call and hope to get a chance to raise back.

Players close to the opener should tend to call regardless of their hands.

Before the draw it pays to act just as you would in straight lowball, bearing in mind that all players still in the pot will have good hands.

In three-card shotgun it seldom pays to raise immediately. If you are dealer and do raise, you don't need a very good three cards. No one is likely to raise you back, and by sticking to this first-round raise, you are likely to find that everyone will check to you on the next round so that you will be sure to get your fifth card.

HIGH-LOW SHOTGUN

Just play this game as you would play high-low draw. That is, if someone holds a gun to your head and makes you play it, go ahead. In other words, it is such a dangerous game that only those who really like to live dangerously will try it.

Dealing Six or Seven Cards

When there are only four or five players for a draw game the action tends to get very slow. It can be livened up by having the dealer give each player six or seven cards. When you draw you draw to a five-card hand. Thus, if you discard two cards from seven you are standing pat.

Like most forms of poker designed to encourage people to stay in lots of pots, the winning player learns that he needs better hands to play and the action tends to slow down. In high poker when six cards are dealt, you tend to throw away any pair except aces and just never waste any chips on draws to straights. You should also be very careful about drawing to a flush.

When seven cards are dealt you should stay with aces if you are the last man to act and no one has raised. Two small pairs are a good throwaway hand, and two big pairs nothing to get excited about.

If one extra card is dealt in lowball, don't ever play with a pat ten. When two extra cards are dealt, the pat nine becomes a snare and a delusion. Throw it away unless you can stay and make a really good one-card draw.

Two-card draws should be left for the birds, and probably the worst hand to draw one card to would be **7–5–3–2.**

DOUBLE AND TRIPLE DRAW

This is a good game to stay away from. You do get two or three chances to improve your hand, but so does everybody else.

You also have extra rounds of betting, and if you aren't careful, you will find yourself losing a lot more than you would in regular draw. Of course, you can also win more, but not if you play every hand you would in single draw.

Don't draw to straights! At least, don't draw to small straights. They are too likely to lose more for you if you make them.

Do draw to a four flush. You get two or three chances to hit, and while no guarantee of winning goes when you hit, your chances are pretty good.

In lowball don't ever play a nine or a bad eight and don't draw to a bad seven.

In triple-draw lowball a two-card draw to a wheel is far better than to stand pat with **8–7–3–2–A.** As a matter of personal practice I draw two cards to that hand.

With **7–6–3–2–A** I draw one card.

After your first draw in double draw you tend to stand with an eight unless some other player has shown strength and stood pat in front of you. Do the same after your second draw in triple draw.

58

5

Five-card Stud High

You start with just two cards. One face down—called the hole card—and one face up—called the up card.

If you stay to the finish, you will have a total of four up cards, and there will have been four rounds of betting.

The hole card represents a male or stud; the up cards females or mares. (Originally women didn't play poker, and this bit of male chauvinism crept into poker language.)

The game is deceptively simple. You see every card but one. Actually it is both tough and rather uninteresting, but it is the base on which most poker games are built.

In penny ante the high card is usually required to bet on the first round. If there is a tie, the man nearest the dealer's left acts first. In most high-stake games, he doesn't have to bet. He may just throw his hand away.

Gambling-house games are likely to require the low hand to bet. This insures action since he is very likely to be raised.

This is the fairest form of poker since the only advantage

59

the dealer has is that if two players show the same up card or cards, the man nearer to the dealer's left must act first.

Basic Rules

More than any other form of poker this is a game of patience. You should learn not to stay on the first round unless:

1. You have the highest up card.
2. Your hole card outranks any card showing.
3. Your hole card is as good as any card showing, and your up card is a nine or higher.

In succeeding rounds, you should get out any time you are beaten in sight. Suppose you stay with a queen in the hole and catch a second low up card. If anyone else catches an ace or a king and someone bets, you belong anywhere but in the pot.

If you stay for another card you may catch a queen. After this you are practically committed to stay to the end and it may be a very bitter end. Maybe that ace or king paired your opponent, and he will be looking down your throat.

Immortals

After the fifth card has been dealt if your hand is a sure winner, regardless of what hole cards the other players hold, you have an immortal or cinch.

Earlier on all you can have is what you know must be the best hand at that time.

The ideal stud situation is to get someone to bet into your immortal. It is almost but not quite as ideal to get someone to stay against you if you bet your immortal.

We have such clichés as, "Don't bet into an open pair."

Some people consider it improper to check with an immortal. Some games even forbid the practice entirely or provide that if you check an immortal, you can't raise if someone else bets. Those aren't real poker games. It must be perfectly proper to check with a cinch hand and wait for someone to bet into your sure thing.

Furthermore, there is a certain absurdity here. A shows an ace, B a king, C a queen, and D a jack. A checks and therefore cannot have an ace in the hole. Now if B has a king in the hole, he has an immortal. He should not be allowed to check either, and so on.

Livening Up Stud

The gambling-house rule that compels the low man to bet on the first round should be used in all except the most serious high-stake games. Even then it stirs things up if you are playing a limit game for lots of money.

Then, the larger the ante in relation to the limit, the faster the action. If you have anted a quarter and paid an additional dime to see the second up card, you aren't likely to drop for another dime bet even if you can't beat what you can see.

Canadian Stud

This is a wonderful penny-ante or high-stake game when played with a limit. A typical game would have the dealer

61

ante 5 chips with a 1-chip limit on the first round going up to 2 chips, then 3 chips, and finally 5 chips. There also should be a limit on the number of raises plus one other rule: The limit becomes 5 chips any time there is a pair showing.

There are two forms of this game. In the first one, a four flush beats a pair but loses to two pair. In the second and more popular one, four cards to an open-end straight beat a pair but lose to a four flush, which, in turn, loses to two pair. It is possible to have a pair and four flush or open-end straight, or to have something like **K–Q–J–6** of spades and **10** of hearts, which is both a four straight and four flush. Such hands just count as the higher category.

Look at some of the possibilities here. You hold **10–9–8** of the same suit. There are ten cards of your suit to give you a four flush and six other cards to give you an open-end straight, plus nine more that give you a pair. The odds are almost 4–1 in favor of your winding up with at least a pair, and better than 5–4 in favor of your final hand being better than a pair.

The only trouble with the game is that the raises are so many that it becomes a much higher stake game than the size of the chips would indicate.

Flip Stud

All cards are dealt face down and you have the right to face either of your hole cards before each round of betting.

When you are dealt an ace and a deuce, you can turn up the deuce and keep the ace in the hole. If your next card is an eight, you turn that and still have your ace in the hole.

This looks good, but the best players don't do this. If

their first card is a high one, they turn it automatically so that no information is given about their hole card.

The man who always turns up as little as possible misses all the best things in life. If he is dealt aces back to back, everyone else knows he has them. If his first turn is an eight and his second an ace, he is marked with either an ace or an eight in the hole.

Flip stud is much more of an action game than straight stud. A player with an ace up and a deuce in the hole is likely to get out if raised in regular stud. He stays in, in flip stud; flips his deuce and will do very well if he catches an ace.

Pot Limit

So far our discussion has concerned limit games where the same principles apply regardless of whether your stake is pennies or hundreds of dollars.

When you play pot limit you should learn to drop right away with a marginal hand. The bets go up too fast to warrant paying a lot of chips to protect your first investment.

6

Six- and Seven-card Stud High

Six-card stud has never achieved any great popularity. The sixth card does not change things enough to loosen up the game. If anything, it becomes tighter than five-card stud. When the game is played it is customary to deal two hole cards and one up card as a starter, and the careful player does not stay without a pair or an ace in the hole—and should be wary with that holding.

Seven-card stud or "Down the River" is a horse of a different color. It is a fine game and usually a fairly fast one. There are five rounds of betting. You start with two hole cards and one up card; get three more up cards and one more down card at the finish.

Beginners tend to stay too often in this game. They follow the five-card stud rule of staying when they can beat anything in sight without bearing in mind that every opponent has two hole cards (not one) to go with what he is showing.

Aces are still the best cards but don't have anything like the power they have in five-card stud.

For one thing, they don't make as many straights as do other cards and never lead to your getting an open-end straight early.

An ace is only of real potential value if concealed. An ace up will scare your opponents, and if you pair it, you will only get action from people who either have you beaten or who have an excellent draw against you.

In any event, this game—and especially so when played with a limit—is a game of percentage. You will frequently play and stay along without the best hand because the money odds will be in your favor.

Let's study our initial playing hands.

The ideal starting hand is three of a kind. Not only do you have almost an even-money chance to wind up with a full house or four of a kind, but your three of a kind is likely to win without improvement.

You will get this lovely holding once in every 425 deals. Treat it kindly and with respect.

When dealt a high pair in the hole or three cards to a straight flush, you definitely have a raising hand on the first round. In connection with straights, be sure to bear in mind that a **9–8–7** can lead to a **J–10–9–8–7, 10–9–8–7–6,** or **9–8–7–6–5** straights. In other words, there are three different straights possible. **K–Q–J** can only make two straights, **A–K–Q** only one. Naturally, the best straight start is **Q–J–10.** That is the highest straight possibility open fully in all directions.

A high pair with one up is a good start, though not quite as good as one that is concealed. Your hand potential is the same; the chip-collecting possibilities are less. Three cards to a flush or three to a straight open in all directions is also

66

a good hand. A low pair or a combination such as **K–Q–J** or **10–9–7** also has some merit.

Other hands are just bad ones, yet some may be playable. A queen and jack in the hole with a low card up has a little merit. It becomes a trifle better if two of your cards are in the same suit. The worst hand includes two low hole cards with all your three cards being in different suits. If you play with one of these hands you are just throwing money away.

The following three tables will show your chances of making various hands from various starts.

TABLE III

CHANCES OF MAKING A FLUSH

You Hold	Chance of Eventually Making a Flush
Three cards of one suit	.180
Three cards of one suit and one odd card	.160
Three cards of one suit and two odd cards	.042
Four cards of one suit	.472
Four cards of one suit and one odd card	.350
Four cards of one suit and two odd cards	.196

TABLE IV

CHANCES OF MAKING A STRAIGHT

You Hold	Chance of Eventually Making a Straight
Q–J–10 or 5–4–3, etc.	.190
Q–J–10–x	.112
Q–J–10–x–x	.044
Q–J–10–9	.429
Q–J–10–9–x or A–Q–J–10–8	.315
Q–J–10–9–x–x or A–Q–J–10–8–x	.174
Q–J–10–8	.270
Q–J–10–8–x	.179

You Hold	Chance of Eventually Making a Straight
Q–J–10–8–x–x	.087
K–Q–J or 4–3–2	.131
K–Q–J–x or 4–3–2–x	.076
A–K–Q or 3–2–A	.072
A–K–Q–x or 3–2–A–x	.040

TABLE V

CHANCE OF MAKING A FULL HOUSE OR BETTER

You Hold	Chance of Eventually Making a Full House or Better
Three of a kind	.402
Three of a kind and one odd card	.389
Three of a kind and two odd cards	.333
Three of a kind and three odd cards	.217
Pair and an odd card	.073
Pair and two odd cards	.051
Pair and three odd cards	.026
Two pairs	.196
Two pairs and an odd card	.124
Two pairs and two odd cards	.087

Chance of making four of a kind
starting with three of a kind is .082.

Don't let these tables scare you and don't feel that you have to memorize them. Just look at them to see how a good fourth card helps you and a bad fourth card hurts you.

As an example, if you are dealt **Q–J–10** and catch any card from a **2** to a **7**, your chance to make a straight has dropped from almost one in five to one in nine. Your playble hand has become a quick throw away.

68

Add a **K** or **9,** and it is less than 7–5 against your making a straight. You have acquired a through ticket unless you decide that your straight isn't going to win if you do make it.

If you pair one of your three cards, your hand continues to be playable although a celebration is not called for. Similarly, it does not pay to give value to three cards to a flush after your fourth card has been of another suit.

Going one step further when your fifth card hits, if you don't have four cards to a flush or open-end straight or a high pair, you don't have much of a hand. Get out and wait for the next hand.

In this game it is most important to keep track of the cards shown by the other players. The odds given in the preceding tables are all based on your hand only. If a lot of cards you need appear, your odds go way down. If none appear, they go up.

Then, know your opponents. If a liberal player stays with a five spot up, catches a queen, and starts betting, you must assume that he has made a pair of queens but not that he has made queens and fives or three queens. If a tight player does the same, just mark him with at least two pair.

Bluffs and Half Bluffs

The winning player makes very few bluffs. He is too likely to be called. Half bluffs are a different matter.

Suppose you start with a nine up and a jack and a ten in the hole. You catch an eight and naturally stay for the next card, which happens to be a jack. You have made a pair of jacks and still have your open-end straight to draw to. If you bet now, no one is going to raise you. Maybe

69

everyone will drop. If you are called, you can check on the next round, if you catch a bad card, or bet if you catch a good one. These half bluffs are sometimes called "Betting on the come."

A word of caution here—don't bet on the come when it looks as if you may make your hand and still lose.

7

High-low Split·

Some poker players hate high-low split and won't play it. Others prefer it to either straight high or straight low.

If you are getting your first introduction to high-low split, take care. It is a tough game. True, there are two winners in most pots, though not in every pot. Sometimes one hand wins it all.

Make sure you familiarize yourself with all the rules of the game. Do cards speak for themselves? Do the players declare for high, for low, or for both high and low?

Is ace played as both high and low? Can a pair of aces be counted as the highest pair for high and the lowest pair for low? What is the lowest possible hand?

Declaration high-low is a very tough game and is not recommended for penny ante. Not only does it greatly increase the percentage in favor of the more experienced players, but it also slows the tempo of the game and leads to many fewer pots. Even in high-stake games, that slowdown gets so pronounced that I know of one game where a two-minute timer is used to stop players thinking for more than that two minutes.

I will come back to declaration later on. Meanwhile, the discussion will be about cards speaking; ace both high and low and **5–4–3–2–A** the lowest possible hand.

The Two Basic Principles of High-low

The first one is to play for low. There is a mighty sound reason for this. When you play three of a kind or two pair for high, some low player may make a straight or flush to beat you both ways, but your high cards aren't ever going to take his low from him.

The second one is to recognize the power of the ace. A very good low hand such as **6–4–3–2–A** wins both ways from a player who is trying to win low with **7–5–4–3–2.** In other words, one ace can win the whole pot. Two aces beat any other pair for both high and low. So if you don't have an ace in your hand, be very cautious about getting involved in a big pot.

High-low Draw

Any high pat hand is a good one. A full house won't win low for you, but it will take home the high half of the pot nearly all the time. As for a straight or flush, it is also a good high hand and may take the whole pot if everyone else winds up with a pair.

Three of a kind is worth a play, but don't feel that lady luck hates you because your three of a kind winds up in the ash can.

Two pair is also playable, but it is definitely not worth your while to get into a raised pot with two pair. As for

72

one pair, just chuck it in the discard pile unless it happens to be a pair of aces.

How about low hands? A pat seven or better is worth a strong play. A pat eight is also a good hand. As for a pat nine, you are in the danger zone. Conservative players don't bother with them at all, and a liberal player should not stay in a raised pot with one of them.

A pat ten gives you a simple choice. You can throw it away or play with it and throw your money away.

One-card Draws

Remember the power of the ace. A four flush that includes the ace is a good draw. Even if you miss completely you may find yourself winning high with **A–Q–8–6–3** or some other random holding.

When you are drawing for low the presence of an ace among your four cards is also a big plus factor. A draw to **8–4–3–A** may get you an **8** low that winds up winning the high half of the pot against two or even three better low hands. Our rule for the draw to low is to draw for a seven or better any time; for an eight only when you have an ace, and for a nine any time you don't care about money.

Your draw percentage increases when you may wind up with a straight. Thus, the worst seven draw is **7–6–5–2.** You can't make a straight, and if you do make your seven, any other seven is almost surely going to beat you.

Two-card Draws

Hal Sims is supposed to have told an aspiring bridge player that he played like a millionaire. If you want to play high-low draw like a millionaire, just make lots of two-card draws. Some will win for you, but old man percentage will be operating against you, and he is too tough an opponent for anyone.

You should play three of a kind or something like A–2–4, but most of the time you will only make a two-card draw when you decide to break a pat hand. Maybe you have played with 8–7–5–4–A and there is so much predraw betting that you first decide to chuck the 8 and then go whole hog and chuck the 7 also.

HIGH-LOW FIVE-CARD STUD

This isn't much of a game when you aren't allowed a replacement at the end. By far the best hand here is a pair of aces. Not only are those aces very likely to give you high, but they may bring in both halves of the pot if everyone else in at the finish has also made a pair. The next best hands are a big pair or an ace plus a low card.

The worst hand is a high card up and a low card in the hole, such as queen up and deuce down. If you pair your queen, everyone sees your pair. If you fail to pair it, you aren't likely to get anything except some bad memories.

HIGH-LOW SEVEN-CARD STUD

This is probably the best high-low game. The possibilities are enormous and the action fast and furious. It is the one high-low game where it doesn't pay at all to go after high. Someone playing for low is likely to make a straight or a flush by accident, but accident or not it is going to beat your high hand unless you have been lucky enough to make a full house.

My old friend the late John Crawford was the guiding spirit in a New York game that I played in occasionally. I was talking the game over with John and remarked, "I thought Jones was the perfect losing player. He is in there calling with two pair. Then I saw that Smith was in there calling with just one pair."

John said, "Wait until you meet Brown. He tries to win high with one ace!"

The following table shows your chance of making various low hands with certain holdings.

TABLE VI

HIGH-LOW SEVEN-CARD STUD

You Hold	Chance of Making a Five Low	Chance of Making a Six Low or Better	Chance of Making a Seven Low or Better	Chance of Making an Eight Low or Better
A–2–3	.082	.190	.333	.476
A–2–3–x	.052	.112	.209	.324
A–2–3–x–x	.015	.044	.089	.148
A–2–3–4	.235	.429	.587	.713
A–2–3–4–x	.165	.315	.450	.570
A–2–3–4–x–x	.087	.174	.261	.348

I have used **A–2–3**, but the probabilities are the same with **A–2–4, A–2–5, A–3–4, A–3–5, A–4–5, 2–3–4, 2–3–5, 2–4–5** or **3–4–5.**

When you hold a six you can't make a wheel, but your chances for a six, seven, or eight are the same, etc.

The higher your three low cards, the poorer your potential six, seven, or eight low. When you start with **A–2–3**

75

you can make an **A–2–3–4–8;** when you start with **6–7–8** the best eight you can make is **A–2–6–7–8.**

The really important feature of this table is that it shows how much your chances improve if you hit a good fourth card and go down if you hit a bad fourth card.

A pretty good rule is to drop with a bad fourth card if anyone who shows two good up cards bets, and to drop when both your fourth and fifth cards have been bad ones if anyone with one good up card acts against you.

Almost all of these low combinations may develop into straights for potential high hands, and some will develop into flushes for better high hands. To see what your chances are, check back to Tables III and IV on pp. 67–68.

Thus, in considering doubtful four-card holdings, something like **K–3–4–5** gives you lots of high potential if three of those four cards are in the same suit.

DECLARATION HIGH-LOW

This form of high-low is not recommended to anyone who doesn't want to work at his poker. It is a tough game —a complicated game—and one in which the poor player is certain to be murdered. Still, if you do play it, you can get a lot of fun out of it.

There are numerous ways to declare, but I am going to discuss only the one in which players declare simultaneously by means of chips or markers. In general, a white chip is for low; a colored chip for high. You place your chip in your hand and hold it out. When all players are ready the hands are opened.

A player who wants to try for both high and low does so by either showing an empty hand or one chip of each color.

In table-stakes games where there may be one or several side pots, a player may declare differently for each pot he is in.

Why should you ever want to do this? Here's an example. The game is five-card stud. You show **9–6–4–2** and have a **9** in the hole. You have been representing low all along, but on the fifth card a player who is only involved in the center pot shows a pair of tens. The one other player who is involved in a side pot with you now shows **J–4–3–2**.

You have to declare low in the center since the man with the **10–10** showing is forced to go high. You aren't going to get anything out of the center unless the other player has a pair of jacks, but any chance is better than no chance.

On the other hand, you are surely going to declare high for the side pot and expect to win all of it should your opponent declare high also.

In declaring high-low, if all players declare the same way, the man who wins that way takes the whole pot. If there are just two players and they declare opposite ways, the pot is split.

This leads to lots of amusing situations. I have seen plenty of occasions when the man who declared high had the low hand while the man who declared low had the high hand.

Declaring Both High and Low

If you declare both ways and win both ways, you get a nice reward. You take in the entire pot. Therefore, if you don't win both ways you are penalized. You get nothing if you are beaten either way.

Ties

A player declares high-low. He wins one way and ties for the other. In a few games he still gets nothing, but the correct rule is that he gets three quarters of the pot. The half he has won outright plus half of the part he has tied for.

Backing In

Player A declares high-low and wins low only. Player B declares high and wins high. Player C declares low and is beaten but claims half the pot anyway. What is the rule?

This is strictly a matter of local option. Some games give the man with high the entire pot; others give the low half to the man who declared low. My own preference is for a compromise. Give the man who declared both ways nothing but split the low half between the other two.

After Bets

It is sometimes provided that there be a round of betting after everyone has declared. This is another gimmick to increase the expert's advantage.

When you play high-low draw poker with declaration you are practically steering blind in a fog. The best thing to bear in mind is that a pat low hand should be an eight or better, and that the best draws are to two-way hands such as a low straight or a four flush consisting of low cards.

The only pair worth anything at all is a pair of aces, and it isn't worth much. Not only is it quite probable to run into a straight or flush made by a man trying for low, but if your pair isn't aces that same man may well ruin his low hand by pairing an ace and take high away from you.

There is one classic play in this game. When a man stands pat he is usually playing a low hand. There are 57,344 possible eight lows or better as against 19,716 straights or better. Of those low hands, 4 will also be a straight flush, 52 a flush and 4,040 a straight, but as you can see the odds are almost 2–1 that a pat hand is a low hand. The odds go up a lot further when people stand pat with nine lows. There are 71,680 hands that are exactly a nine low.

So, if you are in against one man and you hold three of a kind, stand pat. If he is drawing to a low hand, he may well declare high against your surprise call of high.

The best declaring high-low game is five-card stud. The ace is so powerful in this game that if you play it, make sure that the ace is either high or low but not both.

Let's play the ace low and see what can happen in a good game. Suppose you are dealt a king up and a low hole card. Either throw the hand right away or plan to represent kings back to back.

A king in the hole and a low card up is a different proposition. Now, if you continue to catch low cards but get a king as your last one, you are going to win high and maybe the entire pot in the event that the one man who has been playing against you has a moderate-size pair and declares high also.

When you have four low cards and catch that king as your last card, your best play is to fold your hand and abandon any hope of winning any part of that pot.

Should you stay for the showdown—out of general mulishness or because the pot is so large that you want to be in the showdown—you can declare high and hope that no one has a pair, or low and hope that everyone has a pair.

Then, there is a last resort. You can smile sweetly, do some raising of your own, and convince the other players that the king has paired you.

This sort of audacity isn't likely to be successful, but it does have one fine side effect. Your reputation as a bluffer builds up, and when you do pair a king in the hole you should collect splendid dividends.

SEVEN-CARD HIGH-LOW DECLARE

The best start in this game is a low three of a kind. The best set of trips is three fives since there is only one five spot left for the other players, and there is just no way that a man going for low can make a straight without a five in his hand.

If you start getting more low cards, you may wind up with a low hand; most of the time you will have an apparent low hand.

If you do make a low, you can declare high-low. If you don't make a low, you will declare for high only—but are still likely to win the whole pot.

Greed in this game can be a terrible thing. Suppose you have a sure low and a straight has been formed also. You can be sure that all opponents are going to be declaring for high. Should you settle for half the pot or try for the whole thing?

80

Summary

Maybe you think I have been suggesting that you play conservatively. You are right! I have been doing just that. Once you get started in a high-low pot you are likely to want to stay to the finish. That hope that springs eternal doesn't pay the rent.

So, don't get in with bad hands.

8

Hold'em

Hold'em is a rather new poker game that probably was developed in southern Texas. At least I know that professional gamblers around Corpus Christi were playing it regularly in the thirties, and I know that in Las Vegas, where Hold'em is getting more play than any other form of poker, it is usually called "Texas Hold'em." Incidentally, that Corpus Christi game was a dog-eat-dog affair except for a few drop-ins who played occasionally and lost. It also included one curly-haired wolf.

The wolf was a local banker, but since his bank was successful and he was both president and owner there was no one to keep him from playing his favorite game and he just beat the gamblers badly. I never played in that game, but I played a lot of bridge with him, and he told me how to play Hold'em way back when hardly anyone played it.

The Game Itself

Each player is dealt two cards. There is a round of betting followed by what is called "the flop" in Nevada and "the turn" in Texas and most other places.

The turn consists of three cards faced in the center. They belong to all the players left in the pot. There is another round of betting followed by the turn of a fourth card, a third round of betting followed by the turn of a fifth card, the final bets, and showdown.

Burning Cards

In Hold'em it is customary to "burn" the top card of the stack before turning the center cards. You burn a card by dealing it face down. Of course, it is permanently out of play. The reason for this is to reduce the advantage of any sharp-eyed player who has seen that top card.

Number of Players

In theory twenty-one people can play Hold'em. Forty-two cards go to them, three cards are burned, five turned up in the center, and two are left over. In practice, a full Hold'em table has seven to ten players.

Conditions of the Game

The most popular Las Vegas game requires a 1-chip ante by each player. The man to the dealer's left opens blind for 10 chips. The players drop, call, or raise in turn. The first raise must be for 10 chips and subsequent raises on the first round and all second-round bets or raises must be for 20 chips. Third- and fourth-round bets and raises must be for 40 chips. There is a maximum of five raises per round.

This is a mighty fast game. If all possible raises are

made, it costs 100 chips on the first round; 120 on the second, and 240 on each of the last two rounds. Add 1 chip for your ante, and you may have to pay 701 chips to get to the showdown.

Not that you see many maximum pots, but you will find yourself frequently paying out 400 or 500 chips on one hand. Even at a penny a chip, the game can be expensive.

Know just what hands can beat you. In other words, you must know the possibilities when two hidden cards are combined with five known cards.

Here they are: When three cards to a straight flush appear, it is always possible that someone will have that straight flush.

When three of a kind hit the table, the man with the fourth has a lock. If no one has that beautiful card, then the best hand is a pair of aces which will produce a full house with aces as the filling pair, except that if a card higher than the trips hits the center, someone might just have a pair to match that high card.

When two pair show up, two fours of a kind are possible as are lots of full houses. When one pair appears, four of a kind and full houses are possible; when three cards of the same suit appear, anyone who is playing two cards of that suit has a flush; if no three cards in the same suit hit the table, there are no flushes possible. Similarly, when three cards in the center can fit into a straight, a straight may be out.

Finally with a center such as:

AS–KD–9H–7C–3S the best possible hand is three aces. No one can have a pat hand of any sort.

Once in a while the center or "board" will make everyone in the pot tie. An example is **A–K–Q–J–10** with no possible flush. Everyone has an ace-high straight, and no one can do any better.

A Sample Hand

You are the dealer and raise with the king and queen of hearts. The blind opener raises back and two people stay for the raises. You just call. The turn is **A–J–4** of hearts, and you have the best possible hand. The opener bets right out. Both players call and everyone stays for your raise. Another four spot is turned!

The opener bets. The first man calls and the second man raises. What should you do?

Throw your hand away. Your only chance to win this pot will be if the final card is the ten of hearts, and this chance isn't worth the investment of a call.

Here is what these players are likely to have, assuming that they are reasonably good players.

The opener's hand is easy. He started with a pair of aces and has made an ace full. What about the caller? He probably has a pair of jacks and a jack full.

Finally, the raiser? He must have got into the pot with a pair of fours and is looking at an immortal.

Position

The man to the dealer's left must bet first on every round. The dealer gets to bet last. This gives the dealer a decided advantage, but since the deal rotates the advantage balances up.

86

Early bettors should check most of the time. Usually this is done because they don't like their hand, but there is no reason not to sandbag when conditions seem right. Later bettors, and in particular the dealer, should bet if they have any reason to think the odds are with them.

Your First Two Cards

The best hand is a pair of aces. Next best a pair of kings. **A–K** of the same suit comes third, and I rank a pair of queens and **A–K** of different suits as a tie for fourth.

Note that all these hands rank ahead of a pair of jacks. As a matter of information, **A–Q** or **K–Q** suited (same suit) definitely outrank this pair. Lower pairs are playable, but sixes or lower are just barely playable.

Be very careful with a high and low card. If you start with **A–6** and an **A** turns up, you are rather committed to go farther in the pot, but anyone with an ace and a higher card is a tremendous favorite against you.

As for such combinations as **Q–7** just throw them away —except that you might play one of them if in the same suit.

Suppose you stay in second seat with the **8–7** of hearts. Two players call. The dealer raises, and after the blind bettor calls, you also call as do the two players in back of you.

The turn is **10D–6D–6C.** At this point the blind opener bets. Waste no time or money with this hand. Just throw it away. True, if a **9** turns you will have a straight, but this straight is very likely to just cost you more money. Surely someone has two diamonds in his hand and is drawing to a flush; probably the bettor has a six in his hand and is looking at three of a kind. And then there are three men in back of you who may raise.

On the other hand if the blind bet checks, you lose nothing by checking. Now the next man bets and everyone calls. If you want to call also, you aren't making a hopelessly bad play. Remember, no one can raise you on this round.

The **8–7** combination or even **7–6** is a better start than **K–7.** or **Q–7.** You may make a surprise straight. If you make two pair on the turn, you have a nice lead on anyone who started with high cards—even a pair of aces. Even a turn such as **8–3–2** opposite your **8–7** is promising.

Good and Bad Turns

If you start with an ace, the best turn for you would be three aces—except for one thing. You aren't going to make much money because even if someone stays with you, he isn't going to raise.

A really good turn to **A–7** would be **A–7–2.** You are likely to be raised by someone with **A–K;** you will surely get calls from anyone with an ace and a card higher than a **7;** or maybe from a player with a **7.**

You start with **A–J. A–3–2** gives you a pair of aces, but it is not as good a turn as **J–3–2.** The reason is that with the first turn anyone with **A–K** or **A–Q** has a tremendous jump on you. The only man you can really catch is one with **A–10** or maybe **A–9.**

With the second turn you have a big edge on anyone with **K–J, Q–J, J–10,** or **J–x.** Of course **J–3** or **J–2** has you beaten, but no one plays with those holdings.

88

In general, after the turn ask yourself three questions:

1. What is my chance to wind up with the winning hand?
2. How much action can I get?
3. What can I lose?

Most of your strategy is based on how you answer these questions.

Suppose you hold **A–10** of hearts and the turn is **QH–JS–4H**. Anyone who bets out is almost sure to have you beaten at this stage in the proceedings, but look at your possibilities. Nine cards will give you the best possible flush. Three other cards the best possible straight. You aren't going to get out of this pot under any circumstances, and with three or more stayers you want to raise and build up the pot. You are going to stay for your fifth card unless the fourth card is a **Q–J** or **4,** and the betting indicates that at least one player has made a full house. In that case, you want to retire gracefully and save money.

This hand has one other advantage when compared with certain other hands. If neither of the last two cards does you any good, you don't have to waste even 1 chip in the last round of betting.

Raising

You raise when you think you have the best hand, the best possibilities, or both. The only exception is when you are afraid you will drive someone out and want as much competition as possible. If you are in second seat with a pair of tens and the turn is **10–3–2** of three suits, you should bet if the blind checks but just call if the blind bets.

You don't want to drive anyone out, and if you do call, maybe someone in back of you will raise.

Half Bluffs

Half bluffs or bets on the come are very common in this game. Take that **A–10** of hearts hand. If everyone checks to you after that turn, you bet happily. You want to be called, but if no one does call, you have taken a pot you might well have been unable to win in an eventual showdown.

Free Cards

When no one bets, the next card is called free since it hasn't cost anything to get it. If you like your hand, you don't want to give a free card; if you don't like your hand, you are delighted with one. With a very good hand you aren't as displeased with a free card as you are when you hold a fair hand. Maybe if you had bet your excellent hand, everyone would have dropped. Now you bet and get a call or two. When you give a free card with a fair hand someone is likely to have drawn out on you.

Special Strategy

When you are dealt a low pair like fives or a moderate-size one like tens, get out unless you have made trips (three of a kind). If there is even one higher card on the table, you are too likely to be going uphill.

Suppose you stay with a **J–10** and the turn is **8–7–2.** Don't bet, but plan to stay. You may make your inside straight or you may catch a **J** or **10** and end up the winner with a poorish hand.

When the turn includes two cards of the same suit and also gives you two pair or three of a kind, don't wait to sandbag. There is no reason to give a man who now holds a four flush a free ride.

You may want to know what your chance is to make a flush if the turn gives you a four flush. The chance that you won't hit on the next card is 38 in 47 since 38 of the unknown 47 cards won't help you. The chance that the next card won't help is 37 out of 46.

Multiply these two probabilities together and the chance that neither card will make your flush for you is 1,406 out of 2,162. Thus, the odds against you are 1,406 to 756, or just under 2 to 1.

Reading Your Opponents' Hands at the Finish

You can't ever be sure what a bad player has played along with, but you are likely to be pleasantly surprised when you see he has far less than his previous betting has indicated. Good players are much more readable and much more likely to have just what they should have.

Hold'em When Both Cards Must Be Used

In this variation of Hold'em a player must use both his cards as part of his five-card hand. And for neophytes there are many pitfalls. For example, you can't make a flush unless both your cards are in one suit.

If your hand is the ace of spades and king of diamonds and four spades or diamonds show up in the center, you don't have a flush. Similarly, you can't make a straight unless both your cards fit into it.

If the final center is **A–A–10–10–6** and you hold **A–K,** your hand is three aces with a king and ten as kickers. A player with two sixes would beat you with a six full on aces; a player with a **10–6** would beat both of you with a ten full on sixes. This is very confusing at first, but time will make it clear.

Apart from this, the thing to remember is that a combination such as **A–9** of different suits which isn't too good in regular Hold'em is worse in this version of the game. Low pairs and hands like **8–7** (particularly if suited) move up in value.

LOW HOLD'EM

This is a poor game. If you do play it, you must learn to play very tight. Don't stay with something like **7–A.** You can only beat a man with something like **6–5** if he pairs one of his cards.

Furthermore, if you do start with **A–2,** which is the best start you can have, and one of your cards pairs in the center, your hand collapses.

HIGH-LOW HOLD'EM

Plain high-low Hold'em is a poor game for the same reason that low Hold'em is a poor game. There is a variation played in the Dallas-Fort Worth area called "Mettoplex" because it is supposed to have been first played in a town halfway between those two neighboring cities.

Each player is dealt four cards. He uses any two for high and any two (maybe even the same two) for low.

I have never played the game with declaration and want to warn against it. Even with cards speaking it may require considerable effort for even a very experienced player to read all the possibilities.

It is possible to have an immortal for high and a sure tie or win for low with just two of your four cards. If the final center is **KS–QH–10H–8C–5H** and two of your cards are **A–2** of hearts, you must win high with your ace-high flush and at least tie for low with your **A–2.**

A–2 is sure to tie for low unless the board pairs your ace or deuce. **A–2–3** is better for low since if either the ace or deuce gets paired, your three will now win for low. **A–2–3–4** is even better since if two of your cards get paired, your other two give you a perfect low. The best start you can expect to get is something like **A–2** of spades and **A–3** of hearts. You have a chance to get a top flush in either of two suits; if an ace and a pair hit the table, your two aces give you an ace full so that only four of a kind will beat you for high and your **2–3** still give you a sure tie for low.

The worst starts are when you have a redundancy somewhere. Thus, three to a flush reduces your chance of making the flush since you can only count two of them; three of a kind cuts your chance of getting another one in the center in half. Conservatively, the only time you should play three of a kind is when you hold three aces and a deuce or three deuces and an ace.

Extra Card

In this variation each player is dealt three cards and throws one away. After that regular Hold'em is played.

This makes it easier to get good starting hands. You will

hold a pair of aces once in 76 times instead of once in 221 times in straight Hold'em. Your chance to get any pair will have gone up to 1 in 6 from 1 in 13. The odds will even be 7–5 in favor of holding two cards in the same suit.

So, don't play any marginal combinations.

Your Throwaway Card in Hold'em

If you are dealt three of a kind, your hand is weakened greatly since you have to throw one away and it won't come back in the center. If you are dealt two kings and an ace, you throw away the ace and note that your kings have greatly increased in value. The chance that another player has a pair of aces has been cut exactly in half. This is easy to figure out. There are six different ace pairs. Take the ace of spades away and there are only three ace pairs left.

Pot-limit Hold'em

In this form of Hold'em you can play very tight and you won't lose much, but you won't win much either. The winning player must play lots of hands he wouldn't think of playing in a regular-limit game. At the same time there are some hands he should look upon with a jaundiced eye; specifically, something like **Q–7.** If he plays and pairs his **Q,** he is likely to be beaten by someone who started with **Q–9.** The latter is a good hand to play because there are some straight possibilities.

The preceding hands were mentioned because one of the biggest pots I ever saw started with a turn of **Q–9–7.** The man under the gun held **Q–7** and bet the pot. The next player with **Q–9** just called and everyone else dropped.

94

The fourth card was a **4**. Again the pot was bet and called. The fifth card was another **Q** so that one man held a queen full on sevens and the other an immortal queen full on nines.

Each player had a lot of chips before that hand. The man with the nines had all his opponent's after the final bets.

The man with the second-best hand complained about his bad luck. "Only one hand could beat me, and he held it, etc., etc."

It was bad luck, but he had made his bad luck by getting into the action at the first bet.

In a limit game once you get started in a pot you tend to stay to the finish. As long as you have any chance to win the money, percentage makes it worth your while to keep on putting in more chips.

In a pot-limit game you are almost always faced with a bet of the size of the pot. Thus, someone bets 300 chips when there are just 300 chips in the pot. If you pay 300 to call you are getting two to one for your money.

You must consider the following questions:

1. Do I have the best hand?
2. Do I have a chance to make the best hand?
3. How much more can it cost me stay to the end?
4. How much can I win if I hit?
5. Can I hit and be beaten?

You have seen what can happen if you play **Q–7**. So don't play a hand with a low card unless you can make a straight with the right three cards. Suppose you play with **8–7.** The turn is **6–5–2** of different suits. If there is a bet, you have a fine call. If your straight develops, you may take all the other players' chips. But if the turn is **10–9–2**, you really should drop. You might make your straight and find a higher straight against you.

My Corpus Christi banker would never play with **Q–7**, but give him **7–5** or even **6–4** and he would look for the turn. As he pointed out, if you started with one of those combinations and didn't get a good turn, you lost no more chips, but if the turn gave you a small straight, you might well double, triple, or even quadruple your stack depending on how many customers you got.

9

Jackal
My Favorite Game

Other poker games are concerned almost entirely with money management: Your main decision is whether to bet (raise, check, call, or throw in your hand) or not. In Jackal, however, there are three times when you must also decide which cards, if any, you will throw away. This is a feature of the game not associated with normal poker games.

The game is five-card stud with extra cards dealt at the start, an immediate replacement, and a final replacement. Thus, if you stay to the end and take both replacements, you will have had ten cards in your possession before you finish.

The game is played as table stakes with a comparatively low ante. Here are the rules:

1.   Each player is dealt five cards. He throws three away and turns one up. The players turn simultaneously. There is a round of betting, and each player is dealt a second up card.

2.   Immediate replacement. Each player, starting with the one with the highest face, either discards a card or

97

stands pat. He may throw his hole card. Once each player has acted the replacements are dealt.

3. There is a second round of betting, each player gets a fourth card, a third round of betting, a fifth card, a fourth round of betting, and a final replacement. Once more, the players elect, in turn, starting with the highest face.

4. There is a final round of betting.

5. The players declare for high, low, or high-low. Declarations are made simultaneously.

6. The ace is counted as low only. This makes it just another card and not a tyrant as it is in most high-low games.

Reshuffle

If at any time the number of dealable cards that are all the stock except the bottom card are not enough to give each player still in the pot a card, the stock (including the bottom card) is shuffled, together with all hands that have dropped out. This includes all discards but does not include cards replaced. There is a cut, and the reshuffled cards form a new stock.

First-round Limits

It improves the game if a definite limit is placed on what can be bet in each of the first two rounds of betting.

The First Discard

There is no such thing as an unplayable hand in Jackal, although there are occasions when you will not stay for the first bet. As an example suppose your five starting cards are **KS–10D–9D–6C–4S.**

In any other poker game it is the sort of hand that only a mother can love, and even then the most doting mother would give it the quick heave-ho if she had to waste some chips on it.

In Jackal you have many ways to play it.

There is the standard play of holding the **6** and the **4.** Turn either one up. The one thing a Jackal player should do is to make sure that he avoids patterns. If you always turn the higher of two low cards, your opponents will know what you are up to; if you always turn the lower, they will know that also.

You may also hold the **10** and **9** of diamonds. Again, turn either one up. You plan to represent a pair; maybe wind up with a straight or flush and win the whole pot if everyone else pairs.

You can turn the **4** and keep the **K** in the hole. Both cards are spades and while the odds are greatly against your making a flush, it is still an extra chance. Act like a man going for low and play along. All sorts of nice things can happen after this start. Suppose that your next two up cards are a **5** and **7** and your fifth card a **J.** You discard that **J;** catch a **K** as its final replacement, and win a surprise high.

You can face the **K** and keep the **10, 9,** or **4** in the hole. Your plan will be to represent kings, but strange things can happen. Suppose you keep the **9** in the hole and find yourself in action against just one opponent. You show **K–4–9–6.** He shows **7–5–A–10.** It is time for the final replacement. You have to replace first and chuck your **K.** He has a **10** low made. What is he going to do? Is he going to get rid of the **10**—probably. So he discards it and catches a **J.** You catch a **3.**

You will declare for high, and unless he is a genius or simply a good player who has seen this type of play before, your opponent will go for high also.

On the other hand, you can get into trouble. Suppose he catches a second ace. You have to bet first and check, whereupon he taps. Or you tap and he calls.

Has he been playing with a pair of sevens right along? In that case if you declare for high, he will take the pot because he holds a sure thing. So you declare for low. Maybe he has two pair, in which case you have been brilliant. Maybe he has just that one pair—declares for high and splits the pot with you. You have thrown away a chance to take the whole kit and caboodle.

As a last sad option, he has just that one pair but has read your entire play. He declares low, and you have lost all your chips.

Dropping on the First Round

Let's start with that **K–10–9–6–4** hand. You decide to turn the **4** and keep the **6** in the hole. There is no reason to drop on the first card regardless of what has been turned by the other players.

You turn the **4** and keep the **K** in the hole. If someone else turns a **K** you get out; otherwise you plan to stay and hope to catch another **K** on fourth or fifth street. Similarly, if you turn the **K,** you drop if another **K** shows; stay if you don't see one.

If you hold that **10–9** of diamonds you should definitely plan to see your third card.

100

With these and other starts you check what else has turned. Thus, if you have decided to play a small pair (**7** or lower) you don't worry about other players showing what appear to be high pairs. You do worry if the cards that might give you three of a kind are showing. Thus, if you have tried a pair of **4**s and the other two are shown, you have no chance to make three of a kind.

The Immediate Replacement

If you have started for low and catch an **8** or higher, just throw it away unless you have played **7–6,** in which case you hold an **8**. *Never hold a* **9** *if playing for low*.

If you have shown a **4** and catch a low card, don't replace; even if your hole card is a **K** or the new low card has paired you. The only exception occurs when some player has made a pair in sight and has not asked for a replacement. In this case, throw your hole card.

If you have played a high pair, and a man who just never holds a high card up unless he has its brother in the hole turns a higher card, just get out. If you do make three of a kind right off, you will find yourself playing against low players only. You will get half the pot at the end unless some mean spirited person has made a straight or a flush.

Dropping After the Replacement

If you started for low, hit a high card, replaced and got another high card, the place for your hand is among the discards. Why try to beat a man for low when he has three good cards to your two? It isn't so much that you are taking the worst of it but rather that if you hit low cards on the next turn, you are playing with three good cards against his four.

Similarly, if you started with that **10–9** of diamonds and after replacing have added the **A** of clubs, you can get rid of that hand unless it turns out that no one is showing a high card. In that case, stay in and plan to represent that you actually have a pair.

Deception

You must have noticed by now that the good player does not always show what he represents. A man with low cards up may have a pair and be hoping for either a second pair or a chance to get in the pot alone with a man playing for high.

A man with a king up can have a low card in the hole with the idea that maybe he can discard that king at the finish or, even better, hold the king and declare low against a single opponent who pairs an up card on the final replacement.

Betting After the Immediate Replacement

High has to bet first on the first round of betting. Low bets first on this and later rounds. Usually there will be one player representing a high pair and several other players representing low. Of course, if someone has shown a **7, 8,** or **9** as a starter, there is a good chance that he will be paired and not be thinking of low.

In any event, the general rule here is to let the high man bet. After all, if he holds a high pair and everyone else shows just low cards, he is a big favorite to win high and is getting a very good run for his money with several players going for low.

He won't bet too much. The last thing he wants is to find himself playing against just one man. He isn't likely to lose high, but he surely isn't going to win low, so when he bets against one man he is just betting to see if he will get his money back.

A Tremendous Play

After the replacement the six players, in their order around the table, showed:

A **5–4**
B **K–7**
C **3–10**
D **A–8**
E **2–J**
F **5–9**

A checked and B, a very fine player, made a fair-sized bet. D and F called, and A, a good high-betting player, tapped. B called, and D and F dropped.

A's next two cards were **8–9** to give him **5–4–8–9,** while B caught **10–6** to give him **K–7–10–6.**

B replaced his **7** and caught a **J.** A replaced his **9** and caught a **Q.**

Both players declared low, and A, who had been playing a pair of **4**s all along, lost the pot when it turned out that B held no pair.

Had B seen A's hole card? Only in his mind. He knew enough of A's game to know that with no pair A would not have drawn but simply stood pat and been sure of half the pot. To put it another way, he had decided that A was hoping to catch a second pair and beat the kings he was sure that B held.

Side Pots

There are going to be lots of side pots in the game since there will be quite a few instances when all the money will be in the pot at declaration time. A player does not have to declare the same way in all pots. Usually two declarations are all that anyone will need to use, but once in a while three will be necessary.

If players declare with a white chip for low and a colored chip for high, they can use coins for other declarations. A penny for low and a nickel for high in the first side pot; a dime for low and a quarter for high in the second.

Forced Declarations

Player A shows **8–6–4–2** and player B shows **9–9–5–A**. In any pot they are both in. A must declare low since he can't beat B for high; B must declare high since he can't beat A for low.

Now let's look at a sample declaration:

> A shows **8–6–4–2**
> B shows **7–5–3–10**
> C shows **A–4–5–A**
> D shows **6–7–3–J**

If A has a **9, 7, 5, 3,** or **A** in the hole, he will declare low all over and win low. If A has a **10** in the hole, he will declare low all over unless he and B are in the final side pot.

In that case, he will declare for high in that final side pot. He is likely to win that side pot by this declaration because if B has a **6, 4, 2,** or **A** in the hole, B will surely have made an unhappy call for low in the first two pots and will have gone for high in this last pot.

Note that both B and A were hedging their bets here. B was sure to get something by declaring high in that last pot since, if A really had the sure low, he would have won the main pot and first side pot. Similarly, A would collect low in the first two pots if B held a pair or an **8, J, Q,** or **K** in the hole.

Fourth-street Betting

This is where the real action starts. Once in a while there is no bet at all or one small bet, but most of the time there is a large bet, a tap, or a series of large bets followed by a final tap.

If you make the first bet, you must have a good reason to make it. If you call another bet, you must have a good reason to stay. In this situation never bet from a sense of frustration or annoyance. There will always be another hand, and you may have better cards.

Let's look at a typical five-player situation. The players are shown in their order around the table and their cards in the order received by them.

Player A **K–10–7**	His **10** was a replacement for an **A**
Player B **4–5–10**	No replacement
Player C **6–3–8**	**3** replaced a **J**
Player D **6–4–9**	**4** replaced a **Q**
Player E **5–2–3**	**2** replaced a **9**

105

Player E is low and must act first. He checks and A, who is next to act, makes a moderate bet. He is definitely representing a king in the hole. Player B drops. It really doesn't matter what his hole card is. That **10** he just caught has hurt him, and he has no business getting in real trouble.

Suppose you are player C. You have a **5** in the hole. You are reminded of the story of the jockey who had been ordered to hold back his horse and finish fifth or sixth. He did just that and, when asked if he thought he could have beaten the horses in front of him, replied, "Cinch, but there were a couple in back who probably could have taken all of us."

You aren't worried about A but are sure scared of E.

You must rely on your knowledge of the other players to make your decision. Did E check because he was sure that A would bet and drive you into him, or did E check because he held a pair?

You must also consider A. Could he have a **10** in the hole? Could he have a low card in the hole? What is the chance that he really has kings?

Then go back to E and A together. Could E be sure that A would bet. In that case, E would surely have checked with a **4** in the hole.

Finally you call. You weren't thinking much about D, but he calls also. Is he some sort of a nut? Or does he have a **6** in the hole?

We will now consider two different plays by E. Suppose he just calls. What does this mean? Either he has an A, **4,** **6,** or **7** in the hole and is setting a trap, or he is paired and doesn't like his chances.

You don't have to do any thinking right now because the fifth card is being dealt.

A catches a **9.** You catch an **A.** D catches a **J,** and E an **8.** The cards showing are:

> Player A **K–10–7–9**
> Player C (you) **6–3–8–A**
> Player D **6–4–9–J**
> Player E **5–2–3–8**

Player E checks and A taps. Since you got involved on fourth street you are stuck and should throw in the rest of your chips. You do just that. You are delighted when D calls also. He can't possibly beat you for low, and his presence in the pot has increased your percentage.

E calls also. It is now replacement time. A must decide first and throws away his **7.** (No surprise.) D comes next and chucks his **4.** As you had suspected he is going for high with a **6** in the hole.

You stand pat on the theory that E will have to discard. Sure enough he asks for a new hole card.

All the money is in and declaration is going to be a simple matter. A and D are going to go for high. You and E are going to declare low. You will win low unless E catches a **4** or an **A.** If he catches a **6,** your **8–6–5–3–A** will beat his **8–6–5–3–2.**

All in all, you have played well and should win low.

Suppose that instead of calling, E had tapped on fourth street. A would probably call; he would worry about the possibility that E had a **6–4** or **A** in the hole, that he might make a straight and automatically win the whole pot, but A would still call.

How about you? You should have decided that you had a through ticket when you called A's bet. You aren't happy, but you are still very much alive.

It also should not affect your decision as to whether or not to take a replacement on fifth street.

One-on-one Plays

When the pot narrows down to just two players, there may well be an automatic division. Thus, if A shows 9–9–6–2 and B shows 8–6–4–3, there is no way for A to win low or B to win high.

On some occasions prior to replacement or after replacement one player may have so great an advantage that the other player should drop rather than stay and risk all his chips. As an example, assume that the cards showing are:

Player A 6–4–3–8
Player B 6–3–2–9

Player B draws first and throws his 9, whereupon A with a 6 in the hole stands pat. Player B catches a 10.

Both players declare high and A takes the whole pot.

This situation is so dangerous for B that if A made a large bet before the replacement, B should not have called, or if B happened to call with a 5 in the hole because he had a chance to make an inside straight and take the whole pot, he should not call a large final bet.

Of course, all this is modified if B knows enough about A's play to be sure that he has been standing with a pair all along.

I remember a situation like that with great pleasure. I was player B and had been playing along with a 10 in the hole because I knew player A's style so well that I felt I could always guess the right way to go at the finish.

108

So, when I replaced my **9** and caught a **10,** I had an immortal high and took the pot from A.

A muttered something about fool's luck, and it was luck that I did pair my **10** to win A's money, but he never realized that I was in no danger because I was sure he was playing a pair.

Here is one of the best plays I have ever seen in this game. Player A had started with a queen up and now showed **Q–10–6–3.** Player B showed **7–4–A–9.**

All the money was in, and A, who had to replace first, jettisoned his **A.** B threw his **9.**

A caught a **2.** B caught a **3.**

A held out his hand quickly and announced his declaration was ready. B was a trifle slower. Then they both declared low and A, who had a **5** in the hole, won the pot. B had been playing a pair of **7**s all the time.

A's reasoning was that B could not make a straight, so there was no reason for him to draw unless he was trying to catch a second pair.

An Interesting Problem

With all the money in the pot you replace a **K** to draw to **5–4–3** with a **2** in the hole. Your one opponent takes a hole card to **8–7–6–5.** You are unlucky because you catch a **10.**

Which way should you declare? If your opponent has caught a **4** or **9,** it doesn't matter. He wins both high and low automatically. If he has caught an **A–2** or **3,** he will go low; if he has caught a **5–6–7–8–J–Q** or **K,** he will go high. Clearly, your best chance to draw anything back except a bloody stump is to declare low.

Watching the Discards and Replacements, etc.

You decide to play a pair of 5s. Your third card is a 7 and two other players catch 5s up. It is now time for the reshuffle and the one thing you know is that you will never catch a third 5. What do you do? Chuck your hole card!

What should you have done if no other 5 had appeared? You should stand. You miss a chance to get a third 5 then, but if you catch a second pair or that third 5 in the cool of the evening you may win a big pot.

That is a simple case. Later on you should keep abreast of your chance to hit what you really want and also what your opponents are least likely to have in the hole.

A Word to the Wise

If a conservative player shows a king, assume he has another king in the hole even if you can account for two kings that aren't there.

Know Your Opponents

I have mentioned this before but I want to emphasize it. If you can tell what a man has in the hole, you know which way he is going and can only lose to him in one-on-one if he makes a straight or flush.

Variations

I have just discussed the game when everyone gets five cards to start and there is an immediate replacement.

You don't have to give everyone exactly five cards. You can give them just two or three, four, or deal out as many cards as the pack holds. In this case there is an immediate reshuffle. When just two cards are dealt there are quite a few hands you shouldn't play. Specifically, you should not play with a ten or jack up and a low card in the hole. Anything else is playable. Thus, with a jack in the hole and an ace up you plan to take a new hole card unless you catch a jack or higher card. Then you throw your ace. A jack has paired you, a king or queen has given you a chance to represent that pair.

Some people like to play with an extra replacement after the fourth card is dealt. It slows up the game and is not recommended.

On the other hand, a fine variation is to deal the third card face down so everyone has two hole cards. I like this game because the possibility of deception goes way up, and I think it increases my edge if I actually have an edge.

Summary

I have devoted a lot of space to this game because it is the greatest challenge poker players can face.

Just look at the options in play. You get to discard three of five cards and to choose your hole card as your first option.

Then, before the second round of betting you get to replace a card if you so desire.

Your third option comes near the end when you have the right to replace another card, and finally you get to the nitty-gritty. You must decide whether to call high or low or maybe both.

111

It is a table-stake game where you can't play tight and win. That is, you can't play tight and win against good players.

If you should play in a table-stake game with penny chips and bad players, your best way to insure a profit will be to sit back and wait for very good hands.

10

Way-out Games

These games range from one-card to fifteen-card poker, from games with just one or two rounds of betting, to ones with more than ten rounds.

In Indian Chief each player is dealt just one card. He places it on his forehead facing outward, so that everyone but he can see the card. There is just one round of betting, and high and low divide the pot. To add to this game's divergence from regular poker, the suits rank as in bridge so that the ace of spades is the highest card and the deuce of clubs the lowest. If you want to try this game, play the ace as high only, and don't blame me if you lose your shirt.

Then there are the games in which two packs of cards are shuffled together so that you can use a lot of cards during the play of one hand without having to reshuffle. In these games full houses are much easier to make, while flushes and straights are somewhat more difficult.

There are wild-card games; card-passing games; double and triple draw; after-bet games; games with extra cards dealt; replacement games; and games where you don't count poker hands at all but count the spots on the cards. I

113

like these very complicated games for one reason: I think I am an expert, and I know that they increase the expert's advantage.

You may like to experiment with your poker and try out new games. If you do, this chapter will give you a brief insight into many of these games.

The Short Deck

One of the players in a serious six-handed game of draw poker is called to the phone. He returns in evident shock and says, "My wife has run off with my accountant and all my money." Then he draws a gun and shoots himself.

There is a stunned silence broken by the question, "What can we do?"

The host replies, "Let's take out the deuces and treys."

This form of draw poker is popular in Europe, where seven- and eight-handed games appear to be the exception. In this game the flush outranks the full house because there are fewer of them. Also, **7–6–5–4–A** is counted as a straight. Here is a table of possible hands in each category.

Kind of Hand	No. of ways to hold
No pair	463,080
One pair	506,880
Two pairs	71,280
Three of a kind	31,680
Straight	8,160
Full house	2,640
Flush	1,816
Four of a kind	440
Straight flush	32
Total	1,086,008

If you play this game, you should bear in mind that the hands run much higher than in regular poker. Also note that when you draw to two pair your chance to fill is one in ten instead of one in twelve in regular draw. Your chance of making a straight on a one-card draw is better than one in five, but the draw to a flush will only succeed seven times out of thirty-nine.

Joker Poker

Every pack of cards comes with a couple of jokers. It stands to reason that in accordance with the spirit of free enterprise they would be put to use in some poker games. However, for some reason or other no one seems to have wanted two jokers. So, we'll stick to one-joker games along with all joker players I have known.

The joker counts as any card you want it to be, even as another card in your hand to form five of a kind to beat straight flushes. Its presence lends little to the game, and in my opinion tends to ruin the game, or at least to reduce the fun.

The reason is that it is just too powerful.

Deuces Wild

In this game the four deuces are counted as jokers, except that it is generally understood that they may also count as cards so that **6–5–4–3–A** is not a straight.

There is a story about two very good friends in a convivial poker game who had a deck stacked for them so that each one was given four aces. The other players hoped to see an argument. Instead, after many bets there was a call. One said, "I guess I win. I have four aces."

115

The reply came, "So do I. What's your kicker?"

With deuces wild it is possible for identical fours of a kind to appear, and identical threes of a kind are quite likely to show up. Some writers suggest that in such instances the man with fewer jokers wins; others contend that the man with more jokers wins; I favor counting it as a tie and settling the pot on the odd cards.

Deuces Wild is nearly always played for high. It is also usually played as draw poker. When you play this game there is no point at all in getting into a pot with two pair; not that you don't have a chance to win if you fill, but rather that your chance isn't good enough to warrant starting your investment in the pot.

Any pair except aces is also a chuckeroo, and aces aren't worth writing home about unless you are writing for money to finance further draws to them.

It is also a close question about what to do with **A-2.** I favor holding the **A,** but drawing four cards to the deuce is only a trifle worse in the long run.

Draws to straights and flushes are for the birds (birds lead a pleasant life but shouldn't play poker). A straight flush draw has considerable merit and even more merit when your bobtail (four cards to an open-end straight) includes a deuce.

A pair of deuces is a good hand. Hold an ace with them, but otherwise draw three cards (except when you hold something like **Q-J** of a suit with your two deuces).

When you do play stud with deuces wild, you shouldn't get involved without a high pair or a deuce; you should tread softly any time another player catches a deuce; and, in general, beware of everybody.

The Bug

This is a restricted joker. It is given full privileges in low poker or for the low half of the pot in high-low, but counts as an extra ace in high unless it can be used to make a flush or straight.

When it is used to form a flush, it must be counted as some card other than one in your hand. Thus **Bug–A–K–5–2** becomes an **A–K–Q–5–2** flush and loses to **A–K–Q–6–2** in another suit.

The bug tends to liven up draw games; it should not be used in low, high-low, or seven-card games, and is an extremely obnoxious card in Hold'em. It is so obnoxious in that game that certain dealer's-choice games with the bug provide that if dealt to a player or turned in the center, it is thrown out with a new card to replace it.

Hole-card Wild

In this form of five-card stud your hole card and all cards like it are wild. Needless to say, a pair back to back is what you want to start with. If you are lucky enough to get a pair back to back, aces are the least valuable, as you can't use them to make three aces. Thus, an ace in the hole with **A–K–3–2** up is just three kings; a deuce in the hole with **A–K–3–2** up is three aces.

If you play low, kings become the best pair; if you play high-low your best pair is something like sevens or eights. In playing this game as high-low split, beware of the good player who shows a pair and plays on. He undoubtedly has a third card of that rank in the hole.

Low Hole Card Wild

This is almost entirely a seven-card stud game. The pitfall to watch for in this game is that last card dealt down to you: If it is a deuce and you already have a four down and two fours up, you go from three wild fours down to one wild deuce.

Choose Your Own Wild Card

In this game you select any card in your hand, and all like it, as wild. It can be played high-low split, with your right to choose one denomination for high and another for low. For instance, in seven-card stud if your hand is **9S–9H–8H–5H–4C–2D–2C,** you can make a **9**-high straight flush by counting your deuces as wild; and a wheel for low by counting your nines as wild.

The game is not recommended as it is just too much work to figure out what your hand is and much more to figure out what it is worth.

Dozens of Wild Cards

You don't have to stick to just a few wild cards. You can make deuces and treys wild or the whole spade suit. Or you can play Dr. Pepper: In this game two tens, twos, and fours are wild, after the old advertisement that recommended drinking a Dr. Pepper at those hours of the day.

Baseball

This is a seven-card stud game that is usually played for high only, with nines, fours, and threes as special cards.

118

Nines are wild whether face up or in the hole. They are the really good cards.

A four dealt up is a base on balls and entitles the player who gets it to an extra card. A four in the hole is just a four.

Threes correspond to three strikes. There are several ways to use them. They may be played as wild, but if dealt face up, the unlucky player who gets one must either throw his hand away or pay a large number of chips into the pot to keep his hand. Usually the number of chips required is the size of the pot. Whatever it is—don't pay it. Throw your hand away and wait for the next one.

A three in the hole is usually just counted as a three, but may be played as wild or not according to the game's rules.

Blind-poker Games

Indian Chief (see Glossary) is the first game of this type that comes to mind. In that game you see all cards but your own. In other blind games the essential feature is that you may have to play through several rounds of betting before you see even one of your cards.

Beat Your Neighbor

Each player is dealt a five-card hand face down. The player to the dealer's left turns up a card and there is a round of betting. The next man turns cards one at a time until he shows something that will beat the card turned to his left for high. If he never can beat that card, he throws his hand away and the next player starts turning cards. Each player in turn goes through the same procedure until

it gets back to the first man, who turns more cards—
provided he is still in the pot.

Played with a high ante and comparatively low limit, this
game can be a lot of fun. It also is a very difficult game to
play well although there are a few guidelines. Let's look at
a sample pot.

A **Q** is turned. Everyone stays for the first bet but
there are no raises. The next player turns **4–2–Q.** He can
now beat that **Q,** but he should throw his hand away if
anyone bets—and someone will.

Third man turns **10–K.** He bets, and everyone in back
and the first player stay. The fourth player turns all five
cards. He can't beat that **K** but he has turned another
Q. He is out.

K–10 bets. All men in back call; player with **Q** gets out
since he has lost two chances to pair his **Q.**

Fifth player turns **J–9–J** and bets. Everyone calls, but
no one raises.

The last three players can't beat that pair of jacks so it
gets back to the **K–10.** He turns a card. It is another **K.** He
bets and is called. Percentage forces the man with the jacks
to stay in.

Note that there has been no raise all this time. There seldom is if Beat Your Neighbor is played seriously.

Card-passing Games

I don't like these games, but there are those who do. So,
if you want to play one of them or are forced to play one of
them, I will discuss some.

The first one may be the worst poker game ever devised.
I have named it:

Ruin Your Neighbor

This is regular draw poker played high-low split with one extra proviso. Before the showdown each player passes one card to the man at his left. Sometimes another round of betting follows; other times the showdown takes place immediately after the pass.

Playing for high, a four flush is just as good as a pat flush. In fact, it is slightly better because you must pass one of your cards so that with a four flush you have nine cards to make it; with a complete flush there are only eight cards of the suit that may be passed to you.

When playing for low in this game if you are dealt **K–5–4–3–2,** you have an excellent hand and should stand pat with it. This will give you a king to pass to your left and you will ruin your neighbor if he is trying for low. If dealt **5–4–3–2–2,** you draw so as to get rid of that deuce which you would have to pass if you held it.

In going for high, a big pair is better than two small pair. You do draw three cards to your big pair and may make three of a kind, which is a very good hand in this game. When you start with two pair and draw a card it helps a little if you make your full house. You can now discard from your pair and be holding three of a kind.

This game is usually played with the cards speaking. When played declaration you hope to be able to pass a card that will not tell the man who gets it which way you are going.

One last word about this game. A two-card draw to low is much better than in any other form of high-low or low draw.

Blackjack-type Games

In these games you don't go for poker hands, you count the spots on the cards. Invariably the ace is counted as either one or eleven, spot cards as their spots, and face cards are counted as ten or one half but not both.

They are usually dealt as stud with either one or two hole cards and the proviso that a player may stop taking cards at any time.

In some games the hand nearest the magic total wins, with the proviso that if you go over, your hand is dead—although you can play through and try to bluff. Such games further provide that in the event of a showdown between hands that have gone over, the one nearest to the right number wins. I will discuss only one of them here.

5½=21

This is a good game. It is played high-low split with declaration at the end. The hand that is nearest to 5½ or 21 wins, with the provision that if two hands are the same distance, the one that is below wins. Thus 5 beats 6 for low; 20 beats 22 for high.

After each round of betting those players who want another card get one, although you can't refuse one round and take a card the next time. The limit is seven cards to a player.

The possibility of bluffing in this game is tremendous, with the added advantage of real deception.

As an example, a five up and a ten in the hole is a bad hand. It counts 15 and is only going to be valuable for high if you ask for a card and catch a six. But suppose you stand pat and raise every time it is your turn. Is anyone going to stay in the pot and declare low against the 5½ you are representing?

As in most declaration-type games beware of the man whose hand is such that you can't tell which way he is going to declare. In general, don't play against a man who shows an ace or a five, particularly if he shows an ace. He can be playing with a four in the hole.

Sometimes it will become obvious that everyone else is going for high. In that case stand with even as much as 14 or 15 and win low, because no one else will be able to beat you.

31

This game is played for high only with picture cards counting as ten and the ace as one or eleven. If you go over 31 you lose to anyone who hasn't gone over.

You start with two cards up and one down and, as in all games of this type, betting continues until everyone has enough cards.

31–41

This is based on the French game of *Trente-quarante*. All cards are dealt face down, and you start the betting with one card per player (a variation of this game starts with two and sometimes even three cards per player). In this game you must stop when you reach 31, and the lowest total wins. Aces are usually counted at 1 only but you can play them to count 1 or 11.

11

Laws

1. *The Poker Hand*

A poker hand consists of five cards. In variations where a player is dealt more than five cards he uses the best five to make his poker hand.

2. *Rank of Cards*

Regular poker is played with a standard fifty-two-card deck. The cards rank **A–K–Q–J–10–9–8–7–6–5–4–3–2–1**. The **A** is only counted as **1** to make a straight with the **2–3–4–5** or in some forms of high-low or low poker.

All suits rank the same.

3. *Rank of Hands*

Poker hands rank in nine categories, any hand in one category outranking all hands in a lower category. These categories are:

a. *Straight flush*. Five cards in sequence of the same suit. (The royal flush: **A–K–Q–J–10** in one suit is simply the highest straight flush.)
b. *Four of a kind* and one odd card.
c. *Full house*. Three of one kind and two of another.
d. *Flush*. Five cards all in one suit.
e. *Straight*. Any five cards in sequence.
f. *Three of one kind* and two odd cards.
g. *Two pairs* and an odd card.
h. *One pair* and three odd cards.
i. *No pair*.

Between two hands in the same category the relative rank is determined as follows:

Categories a and e. The top card. The highest straight is **A–K–Q–J–10;** the lowest **5–4–3–2–A.**

Category b. The higher four of a kind.

Category c and f. The higher three of a kind.

Category g. The highest pair. If each player has the same high pair, the second pair determines. If each player has the same two pairs, the odd card determines.

Category h. The higher pair. If each player has the same pair the highest outside card. If those tie, the next highest, etc.

Categories d and i. The highest card. If they are identical the next highest, etc.

4. *Local Option Hands*

There are any number of additional combinations of cards that are given rank in various games. Some of these are: the Dog, the Tiger, the Skeet, the Kilter, the Cat-hop, the Blaze, etc. The only ones used to any extent are the Dog and the Tiger. They are:

a. Big Tiger: A king to an eight with no pair. Ranks below a flush.
b. Little Tiger: An eight to a three with no pair. Ranks below a Big Tiger.
c. Big Dog: Ace to a nine with no pair. Ranks below a Little Tiger.
d. Little Dog: Seven to a two with no pair. Ranks below a Big Dog and above a straight.

5. *The Joker*

The game may be played with a joker. In this event the joker may be counted as any card, even one held by the player who holds the joker. Thus, four of a kind and the joker count as five of a kind and outrank any straight flush. The joker may also be used with a combination of cards such as **A–8–7–6** of hearts to form a double-ace flush which will outrank any other flush.

6. *The Bug*

This is a joker without full privileges. It counts as an additional ace and may also be used to make up any straight or flush. Thus, the Bug and **6–7–8–9** form a straight, but the Bug and **6–6–6–10** are merely three sixes.

7. *The Stripped Deck*

The lower cards may be taken out of the deck if desired. In this instance, the **A** still counts as a **1** at the bottom of a straight. Thus, if deuces and treys are out of the deck, 7–6–5–4–A becomes a straight.

8. *Deuces Wild*

The deuces are counted as jokers; 6–5–4–3–A becomes the lowest straight. There are many law variations when wild cards are played. In some games the royal flush beats any five of a kind. Or five of a kind merely counts as four of a kind and loses to any straight flush or higher four of a kind.

In many games the joker or a wild card may not be counted as another card in a flush. Thus, there is no such thing as a A–A flush and A–K–Q–5–4 outranks Joker–A–J–10–9.

The correct law when there are wild cards is that identical hands count the same regardless of wild cards held. Thus, with deuces wild A–A–7–6–2 and A–7–6–2–2 tie.

Wild cards may also be considered as still in the pack so that with deuces wild 6–5–4–3–A or 6–5–3–2–A are not straights.

9. *Preliminaries to the Game*

a. *Number of players.* Any number of players from two up may play although it is inadvisable to have more than eight.

b. *The banker.* The banker takes charge of and distributes the chips. Unless otherwise provided, in the event of a bookkeeping error all players share an equal responsibility for the bank.

c. *Choice of seats.* In general, the players sit where they choose, although in some games they do cut for seats.

d. *First deal.* Any player picks up the deck and deals

the cards around. The first player dealt a jack becomes the first dealer. After that, the deal passes in rotation to the left.

10. *Conditions of the Game*

Before start of play the following points should be definitely determined:

a. The value of the chips.
b. The ante.
c. The maximum bet and the maximum number of raises allowed in a round of betting.
d. In limit games, whether or not a player is responsible for bets made in excess of chips he has on the table.
e. In table-stakes games, the conditions under which a player may (1) place more chips on the table, (2) withdraw chips from the table.

11. *Shuffle and Cut*

Any player may shuffle the cards. The dealer has last right. The cards must then be offered to the player at the dealer's right for a cut. If he declines to cut, any other player may claim the right.

12. *Misdeal*

In the case of a misdeal, the same player deals again with the same pack. A misdeal occurs:

a. If any card is exposed in cutting or reuniting the packs.
b. If any card is found faced in the pack prior to the start of the betting.
c. If two or more cards are exposed during the deal.

d. If at any time prior to the next hand it is proven that the pack was imperfect.

e. If the wrong player deals and attention is called to that fact by a player who has not looked at any of his cards.

13. *Card Exposed During the Deal*

a. In stud poker if a player's hole card is exposed during the deal, he takes it face up and receives his next card face own.

b. In draw poker, if one of a player's cards is exposed during the deal he must take it, except that in low or high-low draw he must take it if it fits in the perfect low, and may not take it otherwise.

c. In games like Hold'em and Spit in the Ocean a player may not take a card exposed during the deal.

d. When a player may not take a card exposed during the deal, that card is shown to all players and removed from the pack for that deal.

e. If the card exposed in b or c was clearly exposed as the fault of the player receiving it, he must keep it.

There are numerous local rules in connection with laws 12 and 13. Thus, in 12b and 13d the remainder of the pack, including the exposed card, is immediately reshuffled.

Also if two or more cards are exposed as the fault of the player receiving them he must take them. See 12c and 13e.

14. *Bet Out of Turn*

A bet out of turn is temporarily canceled and the betting reverts to the proper player except that if the next player after the bettor has acted, the bet out of turn stands. Then, when it becomes the turn of the player who has bet out of turn he must:

a. If no bet has been made in the meanwhile, make the same bet he made out of turn.
b. If a smaller bet has been made, raise to the extent of his out-of-turn bet.
c. Call a bet or bets that total the exact amount of the out-of-turn bet.
d. Nothing in b or c above is to be construed as forbidding the out-of-turn bettor to raise any legal amount.

In many games the out-of-turn bettor is not penalized at all. I consider this silly since this encourages sharp players to make bets when their only hope is that such an act will stop some other player from betting.

15. *Raise Out of Turn*

The same rules apply as to a bet out of turn.

16. *Call Out of Turn*

A call out of turn is temporarily canceled, and the betting reverts to the proper player. Then, when it becomes the turn of the player who has called out of turn, he must call if there has been no raise. If there has been a raise, he may call or drop but may not raise.

17. *Pass Out of Turn*

If a player passes out of turn, his hand becomes foul and he has no further interest in the pot.

18. *Check Out of Turn*

A player who checks out of turn must check or call but may not raise or bet when it becomes his proper turn.

19. *Irregularities in the Betting*

If a player announces he is betting or raising a certain number of chips and at the same time places a different number of chips in the pot, he is betting or raising the amounts he announces and must correct the number placed in the pot.

If he places the wrong number of chips in the pot without an announcement, he is deemed to be calling the last previous bet or raise except that if the amount is substantially inadequate and it is clear that the player thought he was calling a much smaller bet, he may withdraw his chips without penalty.

20. *Irregularities in the Hand*

a. Any hand with more than the proper number of cards, any part of which has been looked at, is foul and the player holding it forfeits any right in the pot.

b. If the player has not looked at any of his cards, the dealer corrects the hand by drawing the extra card or cards and placing them on the bottom of the pack.

c. If a player with less than the proper number of cards has looked at any part of his hand, he may play through the rest of the deal with the insufficient number. Thus, in draw poker he cannot make a straight, flush, or full house.

d. If the player has not looked at any of his cards, the dealer must complete his hand with cards from the top of the pack.

e. If one player has too many cards and another the same number too few and neither has looked at any part of his hand, the player with too few corrects both hands by drawing from the other.

f. If two hands have too few or too many cards, it is a misdeal.

21. *Laws for Draw Poker*

a. *Betting before the draw.* The rules for betting before the draw depend on which form of draw poker is being played. The forms are:

Straight draw—Commencing at the dealer's left each player either checks or opens. Once the pot is opened succeeding players either call, raise, or pass. If no one opens the hand is thrown in, there is a new ante, and the next player deals.

Jackpots—The rules are the same as for straight draw except that the first man to bet (the opener) must have a pair of jacks or better. It is also possible to play with other minimum requirements to open the pot. In all these games a player has the right to check even though he holds openers.

Passout—In this game a player may not check before the draw. He must bet or passout. If everyone but the dealer passes, he takes the pot.

Blind opening—The player to the dealer's left is compelled to open the pot for a specific amount regardless of his hand. In some games the blind opener has the privilege of raising if no one raises him. In other games the next player to act is compelled to raise.

The straddle—A straddle is a blind raise of a blind opening.

b. *Betting after the draw.* Regardless of which variation of draw is being played, the man who made the first bet is known as the "opener," and it is his turn to bet first. He may check if he desires.

c. *Showing openers.* In a jackpot if the opener wins without being called he must show enough of his hand to indicate that he had proper openers but need not show the whole hand. If he cannot show openers, his money and the ante are left in the pot, the deal passes, there is an additional ante and the next winner takes everything. Any money bet by other players is returned to them.

If during the course of the betting the opener decides to drop out, he retains his hand so that he can show he had openers when all betting is over.

If at any time during the betting the opener announces that he doesn't hold openers, any other player in the pot is allowed to announce, "I have openers," and the betting continues. The chips bet by the illegal opener remain in the pot, but his hand is foul.

If no one has openers, the hand is over. The antes and the illegal opener's bet or bets remain in the pot; the other players withdraw their bets.

The same rules as above apply if it is disclosed at the showdown that the opener did not have openers.

d. *The draw.* After the betting before the draw has been completed, the players remaining in the pot have the right to draw cards. The order of draw starts with the player to the dealer's left. He may stand pat (refuse any more cards) or draw any number from one to five, except that in some games a draw of more than three cards may not be made.

Then he discards and receives the same number from the top of the deck. Each player does the same in turn, until all, including the dealer, have discarded and drawn.

The last card may not be dealt. If, as is sometimes the case, there are no cards left to allow the last player or players to draw all their cards, the other players' discards and the passed hands are shuffled and dealt. A player who expects that there won't be enough cards left in the deck for him should hold back his own discards. If he fails to do so, his discards must be shuffled also.

If during the course of the draw a card is discovered faced in the pack, it is simply shown to all the players and placed among the discards. The players receive their cards in regular rotation.

If any card is faced by the dealer during the draw, it is also placed in the discards. In this event, the player who would have received it draws the cards to replace it after all the other players have drawn.

If a player asks for too few cards and has not looked at any of them, he may correct the error before the next player has drawn. Otherwise he must play through with the insufficient number of cards.

If a player asks for too many cards and looks at any of them, his hand is foul. Otherwise he may correct the error before the next player has drawn. If the next player has drawn, he may correct himself by discarding additional cards from his original hand.

135

If a player asks for the right number of cards but receives the wrong number and looks at any of them, the same rules apply as if he had asked for the wrong number. Otherwise the error must be corrected the moment the dealer's attention is called to it, whether or not the next player has drawn.

Unless otherwise provided by local rules, any player in the pot may ask how many cards any other player has drawn. The dealer must tell him.

If a player sees one or more of the cards being dealt to him, he must take them unless some other player still in the pot also saw them, in which case they are treated as cards faced by the dealer.

e. *Splitting openers.* The opener has the right to discard part of his openers. Unless otherwise provided by local rules, he announces that he is doing this and then places his cards under the chips in the pot for later inspection.

22. *Laws of Five-card Stud Poker*

Each player is dealt one card face down and one face up. There is a round of betting. Each player remaining in the pot receives another card face up. There is another round of betting, and so on until each player has a total of five cards, thereby making a total of four rounds of betting. In each round of betting the first bet goes to the player who has the highest holding in sight on the table. If two or more players show the same, the one nearest the dealer's left is the first bettor.

On the first round of betting the players in turn must either bet or pass. After the first round they have the right to check.

If a card is exposed in any manner before a round of betting is completed, the round is nevertheless completed. The exposed card or cards, are buried.

23. *Laws of Down the River* (*Seven-card Stud*)

In this variation of stud there are five rounds of betting, each player eventually having seven cards. The five of these seven that constitute the best poker hand are his hand. As a start, two cards are dealt face down and one face up to each player. Then three more are dealt face up and the last card is given face down. In this game, if the last card is exposed, the same rule applies as to cards exposed during the draw in draw poker—the card so exposed must be buried and the player receives another last card after all other players have received theirs.

24. *Laws of Six- and Eight-card Stud, etc.*

It is possible to play six-card, eight-card, or even ten-card stud if you wish. Any particular number of cards may be dealt face up or face down as desired.

25. *Flip Stud*

Each player is dealt his first two cards face down. Before the betting the players each expose one card simultaneously. Subsequent cards are dealt face down and subsequent turns are made in the same way. Otherwise all rules of regular stud apply.

Six-, seven-, and eight-card stud may also be played with cards dealt face down, and then flipped.

26. *Hold'em, Windows, and Other Games with Common Cards*

In Hold'em each player is dealt two cards. After a round of betting, three mutual cards are faced in the center. A second round of betting follows, after which a fourth card is faced. This is followed by a third round of betting, after which a fifth card is faced followed by a fourth and final betting round.

In all rounds the player remaining in the pot and nearest to the dealer's left bets first. He may not check on the first round but may check on later rounds.

It is possible to play similar type games with any number of cards in each player's hand and any number in the center faced one or several at a time. In all these games the player nearest the dealer's left must still act first on all rounds of betting.

27. *Low Poker*

Low poker is played under the same rules as high poker except that the lowest poker hand wins. Thus a **7–5–4–3–2** is the best unless the cards form a flush.

Variation A. The ace is counted as the lowest card. In this game **6–4–3–2–A** is the best low hand.

Variation B. This is now the standard form of low poker. Straights and flushes are not counted at all, so the best low hand is **5–4–3–2–A.** This form is used throughout this book.

138

28. *Supplementary Laws*

There are so many variations of poker that local rules must be an essential feature of all games. The following are suggested rules for some situations that do occur:

a. *Idiot's rule.* When a player makes a bet that does not affect the rights of other players and that cannot possibly win for him, that bet is canceled. The most common case occurs in a stud game when the last player calls when he is beaten in sight.

b. *Running out of cards in a stud game.* Here the best law is that if there are not enough cards to give each player a card from the stock, a mutual card is turned up in the center.

c. *Burning cards.* In Hold'em before each of the three turns the dealer burns (throws away) the top card of the stock. In other games cards may also be burned by local option.

d. *Calling for a cut.* In some games before cards are to be dealt or drawn a player may call for a cut. This practice is not recommended.

29. *Laws of High-low*

a. The laws of regular poker apply except that the highest and lowest hands divide the pot. Unless otherwise provided, the lowest possible hand is **5–4–3–2–A.**

b. *Odd chips.* If there is an odd chip, it goes to the high hand.

139

c. *Ties*. If two or more players tie for one half the pot, that half is divided equally between them.

d. *Limit on raises*. The maximum number of raises or maximum number of chips a player can bet during one round of betting is fixed by local rules. Such limitation is necessary.

e. In games where a player has more than five cards he may use one set of five to try for high and another set of five to try for low.

f. A player may win both high and low.

g. Division of side pots. Each player competes only for those side pots he has an interest in.

30. *Declaring High-low*

a. *Method of declaration*. The standard method is for simultaneous declaration by means of tokens or chips. When chips are used a white chip usully means low; a colored chip, high. A player declares for both with either an empty hand or chips of both colors.

b. *Division of the pot*. This is simple when no one declares for both high and low. The best low among the low declarers wins low; the best high among the high declarers wins high. Players whose declared hands tie, split their half of the pot.

In general, a man who does not win or tie for what he declares collects nothing. Thus, when A declares high-low, B declares high, and C declares low, if A wins high and C wins low, C takes the whole pot since he has been the only man to win what he has declared for. If A and B tie for high and A wins low, A gets three quarters of the pot (half the high and all the low). B gets the other quarter.

If A and B tie and C wins low, A gets nothing. B gets half the high pot and C gets half the high pot and all the low.

If A and B both declare high-low and C declares low and it turns out that A wins high and B wins low, no one has won what he declared for and the pot is split three ways.

If A, B, and C all declare high-low and A wins high and B wins low, they split the pot since each has won part of what he has declared for while C has lost both parts. (I have never seen or heard of three people declaring both ways, but it can happen.)

Glossary

Acepots Also kingpots and queenpots. The same as jackpots except that aces, kings, or queens are the minimum openers.

Anaconda Each player is dealt seven cards face down. He discards two without showing them. There is a round of betting. Each player faces a card; there is a second round of betting, and so on until each player has faced four cards.

There are numerous variations to this game. Sometimes each player passes two cards to the player on his left before the final discards. Sometimes there are no discards so each player retains seven cards and can use five for high and another five for low. In some variations a player arranges his cards in order before starting to turn.

This is a very dangerous game and a slow one and is not recommended.

Any card wild Each player has the right to call any denomination wild, or in case of high-low he may call one denomination wild for high and another for low.

Anything opens Draw poker with no requirement for openers.

Around the World Each player is dealt four cards. There are four cards in the center turned one at a time with five rounds of betting. See Cincinnati, Omaha, Hold'em, and Spit in the Ocean.

Australian poker See Blind opening.

Automatic lowball See Jacks and back.

Baseball A general name for a group of games in which nines are wild. Threes (representing three strikes) are either wild or not, while fours (representing a base on balls) entitle you to an extra card. When played in stud form only fours dealt face up allow you an extra card, and the penalty for a three spot dealt face up is that you must either throw in your hand or match the pot.

Beat Your Neighbor A group of games in which the players in turn face cards until what they show beats the best hand shown earlier. In the simplest variation, each player is dealt five cards face down but does not look at any of them. First player turns a card and a round of betting follows. Second player turns cards one at a time until he can beat the first man. There is a second round of betting; third man turns until he beats what he can see and so on. A player who runs out of cards without being able to beat his neighbor is out of the pot.

Bedsprings A very complicated game of the Hold'em family. Each player has five cards, and there are ten center cards arranged in two rows of five cards. The top row is turned one at a time, then the bottom row so that there are ten rounds of betting. Each player remaining in the pot can add one or two cards from the center for high and another one or two for low but is restricted to top and bottom cards from a pair.

Best flush   Only flushes or partial flushes count here. Complete flushes are best, four flushes next best, then three flushes, and finally two flushes. A really silly game.

Bet or drop   Any game in which a player may not check at any time. Usually played as a form of draw.

Betty Hutton   Fives and nines wild. Also called Fifty-nine or Ninety-five.

Bimbo   Any game in which each player is given two hands. He can bet both of them, fold one, or, of course, do the wise thing and fold both.

Blackjack poker   A group of games in which cards are valued in points. In most of them they are given the blackjack values of ace 1 or 11, picture cards 10, and others their spots. In a few, picture cards are counted as $\frac{1}{2}$. The games are played high or high-low. In some a hand that goes over the count loses to any hand below the count. Thus, in 31 the best hand is 31 but a player with more than 31 may stay in the pot and bluff. If there is a showdown between two over the count hands, the one that is closer wins. When played high-low it is customary to let the cards speak in most games, but $5\frac{1}{2}$–21 is played with declaration.

Blaze   A hand consisting entirely of face cards. With two hands in this or any freak category, the higher normal poker hand wins.

Blind opening or blind and straddle   A form of draw poker. The first player is required to open regardless of his hand. If there is a straddle, the second player is required to raise. The third player may also be required to raise.

Blind opening (*optional*)   A player may open blind, a second player may straddle, etc. In this optional variation, a player who opens blind or straddles blind may raise even though no one has raised him.

Blind Pig   Each player is dealt five cards but may not look at any of them. Cards are turned one at a time followed by a round of betting. The game may be played for high, for low, or as high-low.

Blind stud   Any form of stud in which no one is allowed to see his hole card or hole cards until one or more rounds of betting have been completed.

Block system   Draw poker with a blind ante and straddle. There is a small limit before the draw, and as each player raises he announces what he is raising to. After the draw the limit is the total amount bet by each player before the draw. Usually played with extra freak hands.

Bluff   The original poker game in which each player was dealt five cards and there was just one round of betting.

Bobtail openers   Jackpot poker in which a player may open with a "bobtail" (four cards to an open-end straight). In a final showdown, a bobtail beats a pair. May also be played with four flushes, in which case a four flush beats a bobtail.

Bobtail stud   In this form of stud a bobtail beats a pair. May also be played with a four flush beating a bobtail.

Bohickman   Draw poker with cards counted as in blackjack. In high, aces count as 11 only; in high-low they are

146

counted as both 1 and 11. Usually played with the double deck. See Double-deck poker.

Both-cards Hold'em   In this variation of Hold'em a player must count both his cards as part of the final five-card hand. Thus, you can't have a flush unless both your cards are in the same suit.

Bug poker   Joker poker except that the joker counts as an ace or to form a straight or flush for high and is only completely wild for low. The bug may be used to form five aces, but if used in a flush, it is counted as some card not in the hand. Thus, **Bug–A–K–9–7** is an **A–K–Q** flush.

Butcher boy   All cards are dealt face up one to each player. Whenever a dealt card matches a previous card, it is given to the man who already holds that denomination to give him a pair. There is a round of betting and the deal is resumed. Once each player has acquired his own denomination, cards of new denominations are just discarded. When played for high, only the first man to get four of a kind wins. When played high-low, the first two to get fours of a kind split the pot. The game may also be played with the deal continuing until some specified number of players have fours of a kind. In any event, the number of possible rounds of betting is astronomical.

Canadian stud   See Bobtail stud.

Cat-hop or -skip straight   **A–Q–10–8–6; K–J–9–7–5,** etc. See Freak hands.

Chicago   The player with the highest spade splits the pot with the player with the highest hand.

Chicago Low   Low poker with the lowest hand splitting the pot with the lowest spade.

147

Cincinnati A game of the Hold'em family with each player having five cards; five mutual cards turned in the center, and six rounds of betting. Played either high or high-low.

Cincinnati Liz Cincinnati with wild cards. Played with each player entitled to his own wild card; or with the lowest card in the center and all like it wild. When played high-low, one wild card for high and another for low may be allowed.

Closed poker Draw poker or any other game in which a player sees only his own cards prior to the showdown.

Cold Hands Each player is dealt five cards, and the best poker hand wins the pot. May be played low or high-low.

Cold Hands with draw The same as Cold Hands except that each player may draw. There is some skill factor here.

Crisscross Cincinnati, except that the five center cards form a cross with the center card being turned last. A player can only add cards from one row to form his hand, except that he can use one row for high and one row for low in high-low.

Crossover Crisscross with the center card and all like it wild.

Deuces Wild Any game in which all four deuces are wild cards.

Doctor Pepper Tens, fours, and twos wild.

Dogs A Big Dog consists of an ace to a nine with no pairs. A Little Dog, of a seven to a two with no pairs. The Dog ranks immediately above a straight.

Double-barreled Shotgun Shotgun with extra rounds of betting as each player turns his final hand one card at a time.

Double Cincinnati Cincinnati with two sets of five cards turned one from each set at the same time. A player may use cards from one set of five for high and from the other for low, but he cannot use cards from both sets for one way or the other.

Double-deck poker Poker played with a double deck of 104 cards. All sorts of weird games can be played with a double deck.

Double-draw poker Draw poker with two draws.

Double-handed high-low See Bimbo.

Down the River Another name for seven-card stud. Usually applies only to the standard variation in which the seventh card is dealt face down.

Draw poker The basic game. Each player is dealt five cards. There is a round of betting, a draw, and a second round of betting.

Dynamite Two-card poker.

Eight-card stud Seven-card stud plus an extra final card and extra round of betting. Usually dealt as in Down the River with the eighth card also dealt face down.

Eighty-eight Eight-card stud with eights wild.

English poker There is a definite size to the first bet. The first raise must be exactly double the first bet; each subsequent raise exactly double the last raise.

149

English stud Down the River, except that after the first five cards and first three rounds of betting a player who wants a sixth or seventh card must discard one of his first. Thus, each final hand consists of five cards. May also be played low or high-low.

Fiery Cross High-low Crisscross.

Five-and-a-half Twenty-one See Blackjack poker. Each player is dealt one up card and one down card. Spot cards are counted as their spots; picture cards as ½; aces as 1 or 11. There is a round of betting, and each player who wants another card is given it face up. There is another round of betting, and the process is repeated until no player wants another card, or a player has received a total of seven cards.

The players declare for high or low or occasionally for both. In case two players declare the same way, the rank of hands is: for low: 5½, 5, 6, 4½, 6½, etc. For high: 21, 20½, 21½, 20, 22, etc.

Five and Ten or Five and Dime Fives and tens wild. Also used as name for freak hand with no pair; ten high and five low such as **10–9–8–6–5.**

Five-card final Five-card stud with the last card dealt face down.

Five-card stud The basic stud game. The final hand consists of one hole card and four up cards.

Five-card stud with option A player may turn up his hole card and take his last card face down.

Five-card stud with replacement or twist Regular five-card stud, except that after the fourth round of betting each player has the right to have one card replaced.

Flip See Roll-your-own.

Football Similar to Baseball, except that sixes and fours are wild with the four also being a penalty card similar to the three in baseball, and deuces are the same as fours in baseball.

Four-card Hold'em Each player is dealt and retains four cards. He must use exactly two in his final hand.

Four-card poker Each hand consists of four cards only. The order of rank is four of a kind, straight flush, flush, straight, three of a kind, two pair, one pair, high card.

Four-flush opener See Bobtail openers.

Four-flush stud See Bobtail stud.

Four-forty-four Eight-card stud with fours wild.

Four-forty-two Same as Four-forty-four, except that deuces are wild, not fours.

Freak hands Non-standard hands listed here with rankings. The only ones of any moment are the extra pat hands, all of which rank below a flush with some also ranking below a straight.

> *Blaze* Five face cards. With two hands in the same freak category, the higher normal poker hand wins.

> *Cat-hop or -skip Straight* **A–Q–10–8–6; K–J–9–7–5,** etc.

Dog   Ace to a nine or seven to a two with no pair. Ranks above a straight.

Mississippi Bear Cat (or Five and Ten)   Ten to a five with no pair. Ranks above a Tiger and below a flush.

Round the Corner   **4–3–2–A–K; 3–2–A–K–Q** or **2–A–K–Q–J.**

Skeet, Kilter, or Pelter   Nine, five, two, and two intermediate cards with no pair.

Tiger   King to an eight or eight to a three with no pair. Ranks above a Dog.

Freezeout   Any game in which a player must stop when he has lost a specified number of chips.

Gruesome Twosome   Two-card draw poker with three draws.

Guts   See Passout.

Half-pot limit   The limit at any time is one half the size of the pot after the potential raiser has put in enough chips to call.

Heinz   Fives and sevens wild.

High-low poker   The highest and lowest hands split the pot.

High poker   The high hand wins.

High spade split   See Chicago.

Hillo Piccolo   See Push poker.

Hokum   Five-card stud. Each player is dealt his first card face down. He elects to turn it or not before receiving his second card. Then, before each additional card he has the right to turn his hole card. Similar but not exactly the same as Roll-your-own.

Hold'em   The new and popular form of Omaha with five center cards turned three, one, and one.

Hole-card stud   Stud with the betting starting after each player receives his hole card.

Hollywood   Cincinnati, except that there are ten center cards turned one at a time. A game to shun like the plague.

Hurricane   See Two-card poker.

Indian Chief   One-card poker in which each player places his one card on his forehead facing the other players. Thus, he sees all cards except his own. Usually played high-low with suits ranked as in bridge, so the ace of spades is the highest card and the deuce of clubs the lowest.

Jackpots   Draw poker with the requirement that the opener must hold a pair of jacks or better. If no one opens, there is a new deal—usually by the next dealer and with an extra ante.

Jacks High   In this game the highest hand is a pair of jacks. Any higher hand is automatically disqualified.

Jacks or Back   In this form of draw poker if no one opens for high, the game becomes lowball passout. Thus, there are no redeals.

Joker poker   Any form of poker with one or more jokers as wild cards. See Bug poker.

Kafoozalem A group of double-deck wild-card games where each player has more than five cards, and five-card ties are broken by extra cards in absolute value. Thus, in a ten-card game the best high hand would be five aces plus five more aces as kickers. Five aces plus two aces and a king would beat five aces plus two aces and a queen. With ace low, the best low hand would be **5–4–3–2–A** plus five aces as kickers, etc.

Kankakee Any game in which a joker is placed in the center and is used by all players.

Knock poker A cross between poker and rummy. See Whiskey poker.

Lallapalooza In this game some fairly common and unimportant hands rank as the best hand. Usually only one Lallapalooza is allowed per session.

Lamebrain or Lamebrain Pete, etc. Other names for Cincinnati.

Lazy Lucy See One-card poker.

Left Louie All face cards that face left are wild.

Leg in Pot The winner of the pot just gets a leg. The pot remains until someone wins a second leg. See Polish poker.

Lowball Poker with the low hand winning.

Low Hole Card Wild Any form of stud poker in which each player's lowest hole card and all like it in his hand are wild.

Low poker A form of poker in which the lowest hand wins. In this book **5–4–3–2–A** is low.

154

Ma Ferguson   Seven-card stud with low up card wild. See Seven-card stud with wild variants.

Match'em   Five-card stud in which if the hole card is paired, it becomes wild as do any pairing up cards. A bad game.

Metroplex   Four-card Hold'em played high-low. A player must use exactly two cards from his hand for high and exactly two for low.

Mexican stud   See Roll-your-own.

Mice   Cincinnati with three center cards only.

Mike   Stud poker with no up cards.

Minimax   A form of seven-card stud high-low played by the mathematicians at the National Security Agency. The highest low hand and lowest high hand split the pot. Even the mathematicians have trouble deciding who has won.

Mississippi Bear Cat   Ten to five with no pairs. Ranks immediately above a Tiger. See Five and Ten and Freak hands.

Mistigris   Another name for Joker poker.

Monte   Another name for three-card poker.

Mortgage   Another name for Leg in Pot.

Mustaches wild   Mustached kings, jacks, or both are wild.

New Guinea stud   Each player is dealt four cards face down and turns two up. Play proceeds from then as in seven-card stud.

New York stud   Four flush beats a pair and loses to two pair.

Nine-card stud   Similar to eight-card stud with either an extra hole card or up card as desired.

Ninety-nine   Nine-card stud with nines wild.

No draw   See Bluff.

No limit   Any game in which betting is unlimited.

No low cards   Any game in which a player may refuse certain low cards. Usually deuces and treys.

Omaha   The parent game of Hold'em. The five center cards are turned one at a time so there are six rounds of betting. Hold'em has almost completely replaced this game.

One-card poker   Each player is given just one card. Ace is always high and deuce low. May be played with suits ranked as in bridge so that there are no ties. See Indian Chief.

One-eyed cards wild   One-eyed jacks, kings, or both played as wild cards.

Open poker   Any game in which some of the cards are dealt face up.

Option   Any game in which a player has the option to replace a card at some time or other.

Pa Ferguson   Seven-card stud with high up card wild.

Pass along   See Push poker.

Passout   Draw poker with the provision that you may not check before the draw.

Pass the Garbage   Any game in which cards are passed to the next player.

Pedro   Another name for Roll-your-own.

Peek Poker   Seven-card stud with the last five cards dealt face up.

Peep and Turn   Another name for Roll-your-own.

Penny Ante   Any really low-stake game.

Pinochle poker   Poker played with a pinochle deck of 48 cards: two of each suit of aces to nines. Five of kind is highest hand. Not worth playing.

Pistol, Pistol stud, Pistol Pete, etc.   Other names for hole-card stud.

Place and Show   The second and third highest hands split the pot. High hand loses.

Place poker   The second-best hand, not the best wins the pot.

Po-Bo   A high-low double-deck game in which a regular poker hand and a Bohickman hand split the pot. May be played as High-Pobo, High-Po Low-Bo, Low-Po High-Bo, or Low-Pobo.

Polish poker   Draw poker played either as jackpots or anything opens with the requirement that it takes three of a kind or better to win a pot. If at the showdown no one can show winners, there is a new pot for those in the showdown with the original pot left in the center.

Pothooks wild   Nines are wild.

Pot limit   Any game in which the limit is the size of the pot after the potential raiser has put in enough chips to call the last bet.

Poverty poker A game in which a player continues after losing all his chips. He keeps getting dealt hands, and when he wins a pot he is back in the game. A better variation allows the player to get a second stack free, but when he loses that he is out.

Procter and Gamble See Mice.

Progressive jackpots If a hand is passed out, the minimum opener for the next pot is queens, then kings, and finally aces. Once a pot is opened, the game reverts to jackpots.

Push poker Stud poker in which each player may refuse his up card and pass it to the next man. In some variations, everyone can push the card along. In other variations, a player must pay a chip into the pot any time he pushes. A tedious game but apt to be expensive.

Queen City Another name for Cincinnati.

Rangdoodles See Roodles.

Requirement poker Usually played as high-low with the requirement that certain minimum hands are necessary to take any part of the pot. Usually two pair the minimum high and eight the minimum low. In case there is no qualified high, a qualified low takes the entire pot, and vice versa. In case no one qualifies either way, those in the showdown continue as in Polish poker.

Ricky de Laet Roll your own with hole cards wild.

Roodles A hand, round of hands, or several rounds of hands in a limit game in which the limit, minimum bet, and ante are increased.

158

Roll-your-own   Stud poker in which each card is dealt face down and the players choose which one to show.

Rothschild   Another name for Push poker.

Round the Corner   See Freak hands.

Screwy Louie   Another name for Anaconda with pass along.

Second Hand Low   Low poker or lowball with the second lowest hand winning the pot.

Seven-card flip   Roll your own seven-card stud.

Seven-card mutual   A Hold'em type game with five rounds of betting. Exactly like Omaha, except instead of a fifth card being dealt in the center, each player is dealt a third card in his hand.

Seven-card reverse   Each player is dealt a closed hand of seven cards. Each player faces one card and there is a round of betting. A similar second, third, and fourth round follows. Each player discards two of his three down cards to be left with a five-card hand and there is a showdown.

Seven-card stud   Usually played with two hole cards and one up card dealt to start with. Three more up cards and one extra hole card follow, but it is possible to deal the la⸀ card up, the next-to-last card down, or any number of v⸀ ations.

Seven-card stud with wild variants   Specific cards ⸀ declared as wild. Or each player may have his ⸀ card, etc.

Seven-toed Pete   Another name for seven-car⸀

159

Shotgun   Draw poker crossed with stud in that the betting starts after each player has received less than five cards. In four-card shotgun, the first round of betting takes place after each player has four cards; then each player gets a fifth card, and the hand proceeds from then on as in regular poker. Shotgun can be played as three-card, two-card, or even one-card shotgun.

Shove Along   See Push poker.

Six-card stud   Each player starts with one up card and one hole card. Continues as in regular stud until each player has six cards. The last card is usually dealt as a second hole card, but any card may be dealt face down by agreement.

Six sixty-six and Sixty-six   Six-card Cincinnati with or without sixes wild, or six-card stud with sixes wild.

Sixth card optional   See Option.

Skeet, Kilter, or Pelter   See Freak hands.

Slippery Elmer   Five-card stud with an extra card faced in the center after the fourth round of betting. This card is not added to any hand but merely makes all cards like it wild.

Southern Cross   Crisscross, except that the center cross consists of nine, not five cards.

Spades as spoilers   Stud poker with wild cards in which the possession of any spade that is not a wild card returns all wild cards to normal.

Spit   A center card.

Spit in the Ocean   Basically each player has four cards

160

and a mutual card (or spit) is turned in the center. This card and all like it may be played as wild, etc. Players may be given any number of cards and there may be several center cards.

Sting An extra card dealt as prelude to the last round of betting. See Window.

Stripped pack A pack with fewer than fifty-two cards. When playing with a stripped deck (say twos and threes out) it is important to agree as to whether or not **7–6–5–4–A** is a straight.

Stud poker Those forms of open poker in which some of each player's cards are either dealt face up or turned before the showdown.

Super poker Any game in which players are dealt extra cards to start with and then throw some away.

Table stakes A game in which a player's bets are limited to the amount of chips in front of him at the start of the hand. A player may add chips before the start of any hand.

Take It or Leave It Usually applied to push poker when played as five-card stud, but can be applied to any form of push poker.

Tap out In a table-stakes game a player who has bet all his chips is tapped out. He remains in the pot until the final showdown, but his interest is limited to the amount represented by his chips plus equal amounts from other players who continue to bet in a supplementary pot to be decided among themselves only.

Ten-card stud Nine-card stud plus one extra card.

161

Tennessee Same as Cincinnati.

Tennessee Jed Tennessee with the last faced card and all like it wild.

Tens high Poker in which any hand better than a pair of tens is disqualified. Thus, the best hand is **10–10–A–K–Q.**

Texas Tech Shotgun with extra rounds of betting. At the normal showdown time each player turns a card. There is another round of betting and further rounds as cards are turned one at a time.

Third Hand High Any game in which the third-best hand wins. In case only two players stay in the pot, the second-best hand wins.

Thirty-Forty See *Trente-quarante.*

Thirty-one Cards count as in blackjack. Each player is dealt two hole cards and an up card. There is a round of betting, each player who wishes gets another card, and there are further rounds of betting until players have seven cards or no one wants any more. The best hand is 31; next best 30, then 29. In some games a hand over 31 is a foul hand and must be thrown away; in others, hands over 31 can stay. In case of a showdown, 32 beats 33, etc., but all lose to 31 or less. See Blackjack poker.

Three-card Monte See Three-card poker.

Three-card poker Each player has only three cards. Dealt as stud, draw, or shotgun, the hands rank straight flush, three of kind, flush, straight, pair, and high card. Sometimes played high-low with each player using two cards for high and two for low.

162

Three forty-five Eight-card stud with fives wild; first three cards dealt down; last five up.

Three out of five Dealt as stud poker but in showdown hands count as in three-card poker. If played as high-low, a player counts three cards for high and another three for low.

Tigers A Big Tiger is king to eight with no pairs; a Little Tiger, an eight to three with no pairs. Tigers rank immediately above Dogs. See Freak hands.

TNT Sometimes called Bull. Each player is dealt three cards as in seven-card stud. After betting, additional cards are dealt one at a time until each player has seven cards all face down. Then cards are turned one at a time with extra betting rounds.

Trente-quarante Based on the French gambling game. The betting is as in seven-card stud with each player starting with two down cards and one up card, except that there is no limit to the number of cards a player may receive. Players try to reach 31–40, with 31 the best hand and forty the worst one. A player may stand below 31 as a bluff but loses if any legitimate hand calls him. When all players but one have stood, the last player takes as many cards as he wishes without a round of betting until he stands.

Twin Beds Cincinnati with two five-card hands in center. Cards are usually turned in pairs. A player may use cards from one hand for high and the other for low but cannot use cards from both hands for either high or low.

Two-card poker Played as draw or stud. Pairs are high.

Two out of five   Same as Three out of five, except that two-card hands are counted.

Utah   Another name for Cincinnati.

Vice President   The second highest hand wins the pot.

Whangdoodles   See Roodles.

Whiskey poker   A cross between poker and rummy.

Wild-card poker   General name for all poker games in which some cards are wild and can represent anything the holder wants them to.

Wild court cards   Kings, queens, and jacks are wild.

Wild suit   A specified suit is wild.

Window   An extra card dealt in the center. Usually in the early stages of the betting. See Sting.

Woolworth   Another name for Five and Dime.

X marks the spot   Same as Crisscross.

Zebra poker   Draw poker with zebras outranking all other hands. A zebra consists of five cards of different rank alternating red and black. Thus **AH–KS–QD–JS–10D** is the highest possible zebra.

Zombie   Draw poker with an extra hand dealt face down. After the showdown the player with the second-best hand picks up the zombie and draws to it. If he can now beat the best hand, he wins the pot.